Frank Hallam

The Breath of God

A sketch, historical, critical and logical of the doctrine of inspirations

Frank Hallam

The Breath of God
A sketch, historical, critical and logical of the doctrine of inspirations

ISBN/EAN: 9783337183288

Printed in Europe, USA, Canada, Australia, Japan

Cover: Foto ©Lupo / pixelio.de

More available books at **www.hansebooks.com**

THE BREATH OF GOD

A Sketch

HISTORICAL, CRITICAL AND LOGICAL OF THE
DOCTRINE OF INSPIRATION

BY THE

REV. FRANK HALLAM

AUTHOR OF "THE SUPREME RITE," "THE DEVIL'S MASTERPIECE," ETC.

"*Thou sendest forth Thy breath.*"—Ps. civ. 30.
"*Come from the four winds, O breath.*"—Ezek. xxxvii. 9.

NEW-YORK
THOMAS WHITTAKER
2 AND 3 BIBLE HOUSE
1895

PREFACE.

THE personal opinions of any man about questions of divine truth are of little consequence to any but himself. It is proper and fair to say, however, that in the chapters of this little volume containing the "array" of the results of the Higher Criticism it was not the author's intention to express his own convictions upon each detail of criticism, but to set forth with something of their own spirit and force the convictions of the critics. It should be remembered that the Higher Criticism is an immature and incomplete science. It is not well nor wise for theologians or laymen to commit themselves to every newly alleged fact or theory of scholars. The discoveries and conclusions of one day are often reversed by those of the succeeding period. It is eminently unwise for any one to deliver himself body and soul, as it were, to the power of a novel and specious criticism which he has no opportunity of examining at first hand, but must accept, if he accept it at all, upon the *ipse dixit* of another. Implicit faith in the infallibility of the scientist, the philosopher, the scholar, and the critic is one of the phases of modern madness unworthy of the intellectual calibre of the age. Faith in the infallibility of God, or even of the Bible, were infinitely preferable and more rational. This author was not present at the Exodus, nor did he follow, after the fashion of the immortal misery of the Wandering Jew, the sad fortunes of Israel. He has not deciphered the monuments nor unravelled the inscriptions of Egyptian and Babylonian tablets. He does not, by the witness of the eye, "know the certainty of those things, wherein thou hast been instructed," in all the particulars of criticism. He merely states them for what they are worth, believing that some of them are irresistible in point of fact, and others of uncertain accuracy and import; but believing also that if every one of them were true, "the word of God is quick and powerful;" that it "liveth and abideth forever"; that it is the "blessed Lord who . . . caused all holy Scriptures to be written for our learning"; and that they are "written . . . with the Spirit of the living God." F. H.

March 10, 1895.

CONTENTS.

CHAPTER I.
King Liber... 1

CHAPTER II.
His Courtiers... 7

CHAPTER III.
His Critics.. 27

CHAPTER IV.
His Blemishes.. 35

CHAPTER V.
His Limitations.. 48

CHAPTER VI.
His Ministers.. 59

CHAPTER VII.
His Friends.. 66

CHAPTER VIII.
His Divinity... 77

CHAPTER IX.
His Exaltation... 88

CHAPTER X.
His Power.. 95

THE BREATH OF GOD.

I.

KING LIBER.

"A Prince indeed,
Beyond all titles, and a household name,
Hereafter, thro' all times."

UNDER the mulberry-trees the pick fell and the city was uncovered. Below it lay the sea, kissing its borders with dimpled waves. Above it towered the mountain, to-day the sleeping demon of a past devouring fire. Fierce and pitiless Vesuvius had poured down her hail of burning cinders and rolled upon the fated place her flood of flame. The terror of that sudden hour to the people of Pompeii no voice hath ever told: the fright and the attempted flight; the frantic screams and the despairing cries; the overthrow of the fleeing multitude and the burial in the tomb of fire.

The sea receded and the mountain slept, and the winds swept dust upon the mighty grave. The grass sprang up and grew, and the wandering herd fed there, and the mulberry-trees arose and bore their fruit; and seventeen hundred years had passed away before the eye of man had looked beneath the turf to see that the burial was there. But then the pick flew, and moulded history came to light. Houses and thoroughfares and temples and theatres were unveiled. The mural pictures still adorned the walls. Statuary stood in the accustomed places. The tradesman's and the housewife's tools were scattered here and there, to hand, as though the workman and the family had only put them by to take a daily meal. Now and again the pick burst into a shallow hollow, and careful lifting of the upper crust of hardened ashes revealed the mould of human forms, as though the genius of the great volcanic mount had fashioned them with an art that strangely joined and intertwined both life and death. The very passions of the human heart were petrified. The tragedy of love was there in stony tableau. In one spot lay the figure of a woman with arms outstretched to clasp the figure of a child—the image of a mother's imperishable love, wrought by the burning of her body in the solid mould within the sepulchre of the buried and forgotten city.

So modern enterprise, spurred by a zeal for antique learning, has been busy throwing up the dust of distant lands and bringing buried wisdom into light. So ages that have slept have been awakened. Despite the proverbs of the world the grave has yielded up its secrets and the dead have told their tales. Figures have come to view of men of whom the world knew nothing. Heroes have stood again, as it were, upon their feet, and walked forth to battle and to victory. Histories have been made alive. Kings have been clothed in their unknown or all-forgotten royalty. Myth has been changed to fact, and Agamemnon's throne, unearthed, has told of Agamemnon's genuine life and heroism.

Among the figures of the past, standing Sphinx-like, partly hidden in the sands of time, is one that overtowers and overshadows all. King Liber was the greatest of the kings—the most distinguished of all history. It may appear impossible to assign such rank. It may appear to be an extravagance of rhetoric, a flight into the realm of myth or dreams or poetry. In all the great procession of the royalties which have risen successively through the vast stretch of centuries; of men of royal character and genius as well as royal birth, who have flashed like meteors upon the skies of history, and swept around their cycles as the stately comet sweeps across the heavens, it may seem difficult to nominate a king of kings. Yet this is sober truth, not poetry: King Liber was the greatest of the kings. Not Bacchus, god of the trailing and the fruitful vine, whom Romans called by Liber's name. He lived before and after Bacchus; and so the two could never be confused, especially as men have defamed the deity of the rich, empurpled grape, and made him seem the god of filthy drunkenness and "bacchanalian" revels. And this one had a wider and a loftier renown than all. His history and character have never been unknown from the hour of his birth in that far-off oriental land where he began his reign. But there have been clouded periods and hidden passages in his career. And still the clouds of time are partly hanging over him. But research has pierced the darkness of the past and stripped away the hindrances to sight, and now his princely figure stands revealed as it has never been before; and men may trace the march of his conquests, and see the features of his countenance, and listen to his speech with understanding, and feel the throbbing of his mighty heart, as immortal characters may be seen and felt across the dying ages. And therefore it is to a calm, dispassionate judgment and to a sober, reasonable justice that his superiority appeals. Visions may be summoned of the splendors of the Pharaohs in their poetic land, rich in its history of culture and achievement. The monuments may tell their stories of the mighty past. The Sphinx may half reveal his ancient secret as he stands but half uncovered in the desert, and half conceal it in his lips of stone. The pyramids may linger like enduring time, the symbols of that immortality which was the glory of Egyptian faith, and lock within their cavernous breasts the royal mummies which in hardened silence proclaim the resurrection of the body. Armies and thrones and palaces and temples may stand in magnificent array, to tell of splendor and power and wisdom, matchless in their age and dazzling future ages. But King Liber had a wider realm, a greater power, a statelier magnificence, a loftier wisdom and enlightenment.

Imagination may revel in the pictures of the empires of the earth. It may picture Alexander in the flood of his youthful brilliancy conquering nation after nation, until insatiate ambition had wrung tears, in curious paradox, from the flashing, martial eyes. It may see the mighty Cæsars shaking the nations with their mailed hands, and treading them beneath their feet with victorious armies, and building up the empire with the vigor of the Roman arms, and with the wisdom of the Roman sages, and with the symmetry and strength of Roman law, and with the culture of their poets and orators and statesmen, until the "Eternal City" had become "the mistress of the world." Imagination may portray the rising glories of Charlemagne bedimming those of fallen Rome, consolidating government, enriching justice, and spreading learning abroad throughout his realms; or Alfred of England, in his goodness and greatness, laying the foundations, as a master builder among kings, of the grandest of modern kingdoms; or Cœur de Lion, in his chivalry and faith, fighting for the sepulchre of the Monarch of all life. But King Liber has blotted out the boundary-lines of nations, and conquered all the worlds, and built up the empire of all time. His laws have shaped the legislation of all future history. His dominion has stretched across the centuries. His wisdom is like the wisdom of the Infinite. His culture is the culture of eternity. He has conquered souls, not territory. He has won for himself an everlasting honor and renown. His reign will never end.

The poets said he was the child of God; and saints and pilgrims have caught up the rhythm of their song and sung it through the centuries. But he was not a god. Yet men gave him an apotheosis. As the greatest of the emperors, though he was never decorated with the title of Augustus, because he was essentially august they crowned him, not with bay and olive, nor with gold and flashing jewels, but with the crown of reverence and praise; and they fell down and worshipped him. And the imperial gods of ancient Rome never looked so royal in imperial purple and resplendent diadems.

They never won such worship in the pomp of their living power or in the lavish magnificence of those royal sepulchres which became their shrines.

King Liber saw the beginnings of his life in the land of Moab or of Canaan, it is said, three thousand years ago. He lives and reigns to-day. Let us look into his face and history.

King Liber, translated into English, is the Bible, or the Book. And the Bible has been enthroned and worshipped; yes, worshipped. It is a curious piece of history, but it is true; the Bible has been practically worshipped, for centuries past, in the gathered volume, and, before the gathering of the volume, in the earlier books. There was never any shrine or idol that had more superstitious homage. There was never any charm or relic, blessed to avert disaster, which had, in men's opinions, a greater power to swerve the bullet from the heart or turn the edge of the sword. There was never any oracle which men more blindly sought, or looked to more submissively for judgment. Its power has been unparalleled in its range of time and territory. Its worshippers have been among the leading races of mankind; among the most intelligent and enlightened people; among the disciples of the most exalted religion in the world. It has been invested with supreme authority in every line and precept, in every metaphor and illustration, in every word and syllable, in every jot and tittle. It has stood, as Herod stood, "gorgeously arrayed," resplendent and dazzling by its superb presence, until men shouted, "It is the voice of a god, and not of"—a book.

In the highest Christian culture of to-day there is reverence as high and honor as profound for the eternal truths of Scripture, and there is worship as devout for their divine Source, as ever in the ages past. Let it not be thought that in speaking of the superstitious folly of men there is a breath of irreverence toward God or dishonor to his incomparable Word. There is reverence to-day, wise and discriminating. But there is also a blind fanaticism, lingering after the ages of darkness, which converts the Bible into a fetish as absolute and awful, as preposterous and vain, as was ever made by heathen hands on the banks of the Congo or the Nile. And all because the Bible has been thought to be inspired, which seemed to mean handed down, in part at least, from heaven; written with the hand of Deity; written under the divine dictation, when men became machines and lost their personality, when every human element was snatched from the writers except the guiding of the pen across the shining parchment, when human souls were practically dumb and dead, and the Spirit of the Godhead usurped their place and functions.

Let us trace the history of this *cultus*.

II.

HIS COURTIERS.

"The shadow of his loss drew like eclipse,
Darkening the world."

"To us the imagined voice of God himself."

SIX hundred years before the coming of the Christ the sound of war was in the land of Israel. The Babylonians had come, and King Zedekiah trembled in Jerusalem. The sacred city was besieged and fell. The king was blinded and carried off to Babylon, the people led into captivity. The gorgeous temple, that masterpiece of ancient architecture, the symbol and the dwelling-place of Israel's God, was rifled of its treasures and destroyed. The sacred oracles were lost. The books, which Israel held more dear, perhaps, than any other treasure, were mingled with the wreck of storm and fire and vandalism which followed in the track of conquest.

A century and a half had passed away, when out of the land of captivity Ezra came to work a restoration. He was clothed with authority from the foreign masters, and was a priest of God. The temple might be built again and the nation restored to its illustrious worship. But the sacred books were gone—obliterated! The nation was without a law and without an oracle! What could be done? Moses was dead, and his grave lay hidden "by Nebo's lonely mountain." He could not write again with living hand the precious laws, or trace the illustrious history. It was a dire extremity. How could its pressing needs be met? *

---

* The capture of Jerusalem and the burning of the temple are historical;[1] the burning of the sacred books only traditional. It is natural to suppose that the sacred writings kept in the temple may have been

[1] II. Kings xxv. 8, 9.

8   THE BREATH OF GOD.

History is silent on the subject for almost all of six long centuries. But near the end of the first century of the Christian era the second book of Esdras was written. We do not know its author, nor the exact year of its completion. We do not shut our eyes to the tremendous gulf of time that stretches between the disastrous situation in Jerusalem and the time of II. Esdras. But the author was bold to hazard a solution of the difficulty—to write as sober history a brilliant story, worthy of a prophetic power to pierce the darkness of the hidden years, or illustrious as a daring feat of the imagination. It is a story of sublime faith in the omnipotent power of God to meet all exigencies, and of an unparalleled gift, in

---

"burnt"; but other copies probably survived, in the hands of scribes or other individuals. Portions of the law, at least, were in the hands of lay people. The king was to have a copy of such parts as related to him.[1] "Fathers" were to teach its precepts to "children."[2] Every seven years, at the feast of Tabernacles, Deuteronomy was to be read to the gathered people. And the later custom of reading the Scriptures in the synagogues perhaps was foreshadowed by earlier public or quasi-public readings. Copies of the Scriptures were certainly made, and must have been either rescued from the burning temple, or preserved in royal libraries or state custody, or in the hands of priests or other officers of the church or state.[3] Otherwise we should be driven to believe that the church and nation had committed the folly of maintaining a solitary volume of the law and Scripture, and to the acceptance of the fable of II. Esdras; or else we should have to believe that the entire Scripture was unwritten till after the captivity. But the tradition that the books were burned, and that Ezra rewrote them, was believed by prominent Christian fathers, and in early Christian writings, such as Clement of Alexandria,[4] Tertullian,[5] and Chrysostom,[6] and in an old writing attributed to Augustine,[7] and in the Clementine homilies.[8] Irenæus,[9] Theodoret,[10] and Basil [11] thought that the Scriptures were corrupted during the captivity, and that

[1] Deut. xvii. 18–20.
[2] Deut. vi. 7–9.
[3] Deut. xxxi. 26; cf. I. Sam. x. 25.
[4] Stromata, i., 22.
[5] De Cultu fœminarum, c. 3.
[6] Hom. viii., in Ep. Heb., Migne's ed., xvii. 74.
[7] De Mirab. Sac. Scrip., ii., 33.
[8] Hom. iii., c. 47.
[9] Adv. Hæreses, iii., 21, 22.
[10] Præf. in Psalmos.
[11] Epis. ad Chilonem, Migne's ed., iv., 358.

all the history of miracle, to Ezra his servant, the priest and scribe. It is important to be mentioned here, because this story has spread its influence all down the after-centuries, and lent its color to much subsequent thought about the origin of the Bible. It tells of how Ezra pleaded before the everlasting throne that the nation might be lifted out of its solemn difficulty; and how the answer came. God lit "a candle of understanding" in his heart. The light and flame were of the Holy Ghost. The heart was warmed and the understanding saw; and to the kindling vision of the scribe Moses and all Israel sprang up again out of the hidden past. History and the law were called back, and, word for word, as they had stood before in the lost books, the sacred writings were restored.*

This is the beginning of King Liber's open history. This was the period of his coronation. Ezra "slew idolatry" and Ezra restored them. Jerome is "indifferent" to whether Moses or Ezra was the author of the Pentateuch.[1] Bellarmine thought that the books were not entirely lost, and that Ezra corrected and improved the copies he restored.[2]

* " For thy law is burnt, therefore no man knoweth the things that are done of thee or the works that shall begin. But if I have found grace before thee, send the Holy Ghost into me, and I shall write all that hath been done in the world since the beginning, which were written in thy law, that men may find thy path. And he answered me, saying, . . . Come hither and I will light a candle of understanding in thine heart, which shall not be put out till the things be performed which thou shalt begin to write, and when thou hast done some things shalt thou publish, and some shalt thou show secretly to the wise: to-morrow at this hour shalt thou begin to write. . . . And the next day, behold, a voice called me, saying, Esdras, open thy mouth, and drink what I give thee to drink! Then opened I my mouth, and, behold, he reached me a full cup, which was full as it were with water, but the color of it was like fire, and I took it and drank: and when I had drunk of it, my heart uttered understanding, and wisdom grew in my breast, for my spirit strengthened my memory."—*II. Esdras* xiv. 21-26, 38-40. In the power of this gift, the story goes on to say, ninety-four books were written in forty days. Of these Ezra was to "publish openly" the first twenty-four. The other seventy

[1] Adv. Helvidiium.   [2] De Verbo Dei, lib. 2.

lifted a book above the dismantled altars to occupy the vacant throne. This is the beginning of the history of Inspiration— that mystic word which we would fain unveil within these pages. This is the most brilliant instance of the highest theory in human thought; an illustration of the blowing of the Breath of God.

What shall we think of it, and all its progeny of varying opinion, as we trace their history through thirty centuries? It is not a definition, but the allegation of a fact. The books beyond the reach of human recovery were copied through the direct enlightenment of the Holy Ghost. God breathed his breath, or Spirit, into the ardent scribe. Is it true? Is it true of all the sacred writers and of all the Scripture canon? Is the Bible inspired? Did God breathe into it the breath of spiritual life?

1. The Talmud thought so, much as Esdras thought so, without defining the nature of the fact—the Talmud, that marvelous rival and outstripper of the books themselves: oral at first, supplementary to the Law and explanatory of it, and then growing superior to it in the Jewish estimation, and written down with endless detail and refinement. In many utterances it paid its tribute to the Law as "given by inspiration of God."

And Philo thought so—the Jewish scholar, the Alexandrian philosopher, the brilliant writer and exponent of Jewish thought; among the first of their authorities at the Christian era, distinguished as one of their master minds in all the centuries since. He speaks of "sacred Scriptures," "sacred books," the "sacred Word," the "oracle," as the Talmud does. He speaks of different degrees of inspiration, but says that the prophets had the divine communications in an "ecstasy," and were "passive" under them. "The prophet," he declares,

he was to show only "to such as be wise." The twenty-four were the twenty-four books of the Old Testament, the number by the Jewish computation. Yet at the time of Ezra many of those books had not been written and their authors had not been born.

"gives forth nothing of his own, but acts at the prompting of another in all his utterances. As long as he is under inspiration he is in ignorance, his reason departing from its place and yielding up the citadel of his soul, the Divine Spirit enters into it and dwells in it."[1] He insists that there is "nothing superfluous in the law."[2] Every word is divine. Even Hebraisms have a special significance, such as "blessing I will bless," and "let him die the death." And the little words as well, as in "brought him *out*," and "thou shalt not plant *thyself* a vineyard." But Philo was enthusiastic on the matter of inspiration. He ascribed it to the Septuagint;[*] to the great philosophers; to all good men; and, in rapt moments, even to himself. Plato is the "most sacred," Hera-

---

[1] De Special, Legg., iv., 8 (Mangey, ii., 343).
[2] De Prof., 10 (Mang., i., 554).
[*] The Septuagint is the Greek translation of the Hebrew Scriptures—apparently the earliest translation ever made. History tells us that it was a growth. When it began, and how long it continued, and by whom it was made, cannot be determined. The earliest mention of it is in a forged letter signed by the name of Aristeas, an officer of Ptolemy Philadelphus. This Ptolemy reigned in Egypt thirty-eight years, beginning in 285 B.C. The next direct evidence of its existence is given by Aristobulus, the Jewish-Alexandrian philosopher, who lived in the reign of Ptolemy Philometor, 180–145 B.C.; and the next in the prologue to Ecclesiasticus, which shows that it was known in 130 B.C. By the time of Christ it was current among the Jews—the popular version read in the synagogues and used by the apostles. Afterward it was the version referred to and quoted by the New Testament, and the version used by the Christian fathers and the Christian people of the early centuries. Its name comes from a fable in the forged letter of Aristeas, which said that Demetrius Phalereus, keeper of the library at Alexandria, begged Ptolemy Philadelphus to have a translation of the Hebrew Scriptures made. That the king assented; sent commissioners to Eleazar, the high priest at Jerusalem, asking him to send six scholars from each of the twelve tribes to Alexandria to make it; and that this was done. The fable continues to the effect that the translators were confined in separate cells, and each made his translation alone; and that when the translations were completed and compared they were found to be all literally alike. As there were seventy-two translators—seventy in round numbers—the version became

clitus the "great and renowned," Parmenides, Empedocles, Zeno, and Cleanthes, "godlike men, and as it were a true and in the strict sense sacred band." [1]

A half-century after Philo, Josephus arises to give his testimony—the great Jewish historian of the Christian era; a "Hebrew of the Hebrews"; of high political prominence among his countrymen, and influential at the courts of Nero and Vespasian. "He speaks of 'the Deity as being present with' a writer; of 'holding converse with God'; of 'being possessed or inspired by God'; of 'being filled with Deity'; of 'being in a state of divine inspiration'; of 'the Spirit of God taking hold of the prophets'; of 'the divine gift passing over' from one person to another." [2] He says that Balaam prophesied, "not as master of himself, but moved to say what he did by the divine Spirit." [3] He represents Balaam as though saying to Balak, "Thinkest thou that it is in our power to speak or be silent . . . when the Spirit of God takes possession of us? For he causes us to utter words such as he wills and speeches without our knowledge . . . for when he has entered into us nothing that is in us is any longer our own." [4] He declares that the Jews, from the hour of their birth, esteem the Scripture as the "decrees of God," and, as the evidence of their fidelity and reverence toward the Bible, that "no one has ever dared to add or subtract or alter anything in it." [5]

2. The Rabbins—which is the same as rabbis, which is the same as teachers, masters, doctors—according to all acounts of them, were believers in the highest literal and verbal inspiration. Organized in the Sanhedrin before and after the time of Christ, and represented from century to century by the learned scholars of later days, they have ever stood as

known as the translation of the Seventy, or the Septuagint. Philo believed this fable. Hence his belief in the inspiration of the Septuagint.

[1] Passages in Schürer, Gesch. d. Jüd. Volkes, ii., 868.
[2] Inspiration, Sanday, p. 77.
[3] Josephus, Antiquities, iv., 6, 5.
[4] Contra Apion, i., 8.   [5] Ibid.

leading representatives of Jewish thought. They said that God handed the Mosaic writings already written from heaven;[1] that Jehovah himself was so fascinated by their perfection that he spent three hours a day in the study of them;[2] that "the numbers of the letters, every single letter, the collocation of every letter, the transposition, the substitution, had a special, even a supernatural power."[3] The later Jews preserved a tradition that when Moses went up into Mount Sinai "he found Jehovah making the ornamental letters in the book of the Law." "They were most scrupulous in recording every little peculiarity of writing, every correction or variety of reading; they counted every word, every verse, every letter; recorded how many times each separate letter of the alphabet occurs; told how often the same word occurs at the beginning, middle or end of a verse; they gave the middle verse, middle word, middle letter of each book of the Pentateuch; they would not dare to alter in the text even an evident mistake, but had an intricate method of indicating it on the margin. 'My son,' said Rabbi Ishmael, 'take great heed how thou doest thy work—for thy work is the work of Heaven—lest thou drop or add a letter of the manuscript, and so become a destroyer of the world.'"[4]

And yet the rabbins and the later Jews did not rank the Scriptures on a single level of inspiration. Their Bible was marked with three great divisions: the Law, the Prophets, and the Hagiographa or Sacred Writings. These, in themselves, imply a distinction. Maimonides, a learned Spanish rabbi of the twelfth century, elaborates *eleven* degrees of inspiration.[5] The modern Jews, as represented by Abarbonel, have reduced these to *three*.[6] The Mosaic is first, the Prophetic second, and that of the Holy Spirit, strange to say, the third and low-

---

[1] How God Inspired the Bible, Smyth, p. 50.   [2] Ibid.
[3] Hist. Interp., Farrar, p. 97 (quoted).
[4] Old Documents and New Bible, Smyth, p. 91.
[5] The Inspiration of Holy Scripture, William Lee, D.D., p. 457.
[6] Ibid.

est. With all the Jews Moses, in this matter, is ever *facile princeps*. Maimonides says: "All the other prophets saw the prophecy in a dream or in a vision; but our Rabbi Moses while he was awake.[1] To all the other prophets it was revealed through the medium of an angel . . . but to Moses it is said, 'With him will I speak mouth to mouth,'[2] and 'face to face ;'[3] and 'as a man speaketh unto his friend.' "[4]

3. From the rabbins we look onward to the Christian Fathers. They also rise out of the dim distance and bear witness. It is not infallible. It is not the voice of authority. They were not themselves inspired. They stand upon a level with saints and doctors in all ages; and faith and learning to-day may teach as much, or more, as in the days gone by. But time and distance have invested the fathers with a mellow radiance, and mediæval sentimentalism has crowned their reverend heads with halos of glory. They stand far off from us, and "distance lends enchantment to the view." They stand comparatively near, in point of time, to the origin of Christianity. In point of fact, they stood far off in many instances. A hundred long and weary years from Christ—or two centuries, or five—may as effectually close the door to knowledge as twenty. Tradition revels in inaccuracies. But in the lapse of time a century becomes a unit, and the long perspective, which makes the horizon kiss the sea, makes the units touch each other, until it seems as though the centuries were linking hands, and the age of Constantine falls into the embrace of that of Christ. But still the fathers are justly rich in modern memory. They were among the pioneers and heroes of the cross. They bear illustrious names, and belong to an illustrious line. If human opinion in testimony to a fact has any value, the opinions of the fathers have distinguished merit. Clement of Rome says that the sacred writings are "true words of the Holy Ghost."[5] Justin Martyr, that the

---

[1] Yad Hachazakah, ch. vii., p. 116 (Bernard's translation).
[2] Num. xii. 8. [3] Ex. xxxiii. 11. [4] Ibid.
[5] Quoted by Smyth, How God Inspired the Bible, p. 74.

Spirit acted on the writers as "the plectrum striking the lyre."[1] Athenagoras says that "the Spirit uses the writers as a flute-player might blow into his flute."[2] Irenæus: "We know the Scriptures, as being spoken by the Word of God and his Spirit."[3] Tertullian: "I adore the perfection of Scriptures. ... If it is not written, let them fear the woe which is destined for them who add to or take away."[4] Athanasius: "The holy and divinely inspired Scriptures are of themselves sufficient to the enunciation of the truth."[5] Basil: "Believe those things which are written; the things which are not written seek not."[6] Tertullian speaks of the Scriptures as "uttered by God and dictated by the Holy Ghost." "He will not allow to Valentinian that there are any varying degrees of inspiration, nor to Marcion that Paul's insight was any deeper than that of other apostles."[7] He thought that the divine communications were given to the writers in an "ecstasy" or "trance."[8] Clement of Alexandria believed in "verbal inspiration and the complete infallibility of Scripture."[9] Augustine[10] "speaks of the Gospels as dictated by the Head of the church, and generally asserts the infallible accuracy of every word of Scripture." He calls the writers "pens of the Holy Ghost."[11] Eusebius "is indignant that one should assert the possibility of the psalmist making a mistake in a name."[12] He says that "the divine Scriptures were spoken by the Holy Ghost."[13] Origen, the greatest scholar among Christians of his day, says that "Christ, the Word of God, was in Moses and the prophets ... and by his Spirit they spake and did all things."[14] He "believed in the inspira-

---

[1] Quoted by Smyth, How God Inspired the Bible, p. 74.
[2] Quæst. ad Autolyc., ii., 9.
[3] Verbo Dei, etc., lib. 2., c. 47.   [4] Adv. Hermogenem, c. 22.
[5] Contra Gentes, tom. i., p. 1.   Basil, Hom. xxix.
[7] Bamp. Lec., 1885, p. 177; Apol., 18; De Pudic., 17.
[8] How God Inspired the Bible, Smyth, p. 75.   [9] Ibid.
[10] Ibid.   [11] Bamp. Lec., 1885, p. 237.
[12] How God Inspired the Bible, p. 75.
[13] Westcott, Introduction, p. 417.   [14] Ibid., p. 430.

tion of the Septuagint[1] and saw hidden mysteries in its solecisms and errors."[2] *

But the fathers were not always consistent. Great and famous and full of faith and deeply reverential, the critical faculty was not always dead in them. They sometimes picked flaws in the sacred Word, and arraigned it before the bar of reason, and found sentence against it, as we shall see.

4. In the "dark ages"[†] there was naturally no flood of light cast upon the question of Inspiration. Christian opinion, more blindly, remained the same as in the early centuries; and largely so throughout the scholastic period.[‡] Commentaries and treatises and volumes were but the echoes of the sentiments of the fathers. Questions springing out of the critical faculty were answered by the allegorical interpretation[§] or by the voice of the papacy.

By the allegorical method the letter was divine, but the spirit was diviner still. There was a literal sense, of course; but there was also a mystical sense, more luminous and lofty. The method was begotten of Aristobulus, and matured by

---

[1] Origen, Philokal, p. 33.   [2] Bamp. Lec., 1885, p. 189.

* The opinions of the fathers here given are few in number, but they are fair examples of the opinions of all. To quote them more freely is only to multiply repetitions.

† From the seventh to the twelfth centuries.

‡ From the twelfth to the sixteenth centuries.

§ The use of allegory in interpreting Scripture arose among the Alexandrian Jews in the second century B.C. Aristobulus (160 B.C.), a Jew of Alexandria, is the first known to have used it. Instances of it first appear in some fragments of his and in the forged letter of Aristeas. Aristobulus was a Peripatetic philosopher, and, charmed with the Platonic thought, he sought a harmony between the beauty of Greek ideas and the revelation of the Hebrew Scriptures. He would exalt Moses and Abraham in the eyes of the cultured Greeks. He would lift the Law and the history of the chosen people, even in trivial details of expression, to stand upon a level with the high conceits of philosophy. So it came about that the letter of Scripture was thought to be written only for the ignorant. The learned and spiritual might pierce through the precincts of the letter and stand within the boundaries of a new world of grand ideas.

Philo, and propelled far down into the Christian centuries. To illustrate: Philo says, "It would be a sign of great simplicity to think that the world was created in six days, or indeed at all in time." Six was a perfect number. Again, that "God planted a garden in Eden . . . let not such fabulous nonsense ever enter your minds."[1] God plants virtue on earth in human souls. Augustine says that the drunkenness of Noah was "a figure of the death and passion of Christ."[2] Thomas Aquinas says that the words in Genesis known as the fiat of creation, "Let there be light," mean "Let Christ be love."[3] Pope Boniface VIII. declared that Christ's command to Peter, "Feed my lambs," because kings were not excepted, gave him power to set aside their decrees; that the plural "keys" in the apostolic commission meant kingly as well as papal power; that Christ's injunction to the fishermen, "Launch out into the deep," meant "Go to Rome; betake thyself to the city which hath dominion over all nations, and there lay down thy net."[4] So, in the hands of rabbis, fathers, popes, and schoolmen, the mystical sense became the solvent of every difficulty of interpretation. History, science, facts, chronology, uncertainties of text and renderings, had no place where language was chiefly allegory. The traditional opinions about the inspiration and infallibility of the Bible were the only ones. What the rabbis and fathers had thought, what the pope thought, was quite enough for the inquiring spirit. Gregory the Great, in the latter half of the sixth century, spoke of the writers of Scripture as "pens of the triune God."[5] He was followed by many others. Bonaventura, in the thirteenth century, in overpowering Latin eloquence, pays tribute to the Bible thus: "Its altitude is unattainable because of its inviolable authority; its plenitude inexhaustible because of its inscrutable profundity; its certitude infallible because of

---

[1] Bamp. Lec., 1885, p. 143 (quoted).
[2] Hom. in Gen., 13, §3.
[3] Bamp. Lec., 1885, p. 275.
[4] Ibid., p. 298 (quoted).   [5] Ibid., p. 287.

its irrefutable progress; its value inappreciable because of its inestimable fruit; its pulchritude incontaminable because of its impermixtible purity."[1] Nicholas of Lyra, in the fourteenth century, "repeats the phrase that God is the *auctor principalis* of Scripture."[2] "The faculties of Louvain and Douai called it 'an intolerable and great blasphemy' to say that there was an otiose word in Scripture. 'Every phrase, syllable, tittle, and point is full of a divine sense.'"[3]

The idea of all this period was clearly the traditional idea of Inspiration. "It was confused with verbal dictation, and the Bible was turned into an amulet or fetish with which 'the church' could do as it liked. The result was 'to nullify the use of Scripture as a record of the divine dealings with the successive generations of mankind. The voice of God was no longer heard as it spoke at sundry times and in divers manners to holy men of old, but simply as uttering the hallowed symbols of an oracular wisdom. The whole of Scripture was treated as one contemporaneous production, of which the several parts might be expounded without reference to the circumstances in which each was delivered.' And thus the Bible was degraded to the level of the Koran, and the piety of the schoolmen became a superstition, transubstantiating the Word of God into the verbal elements by which it was signified."[4]

5. But Scholasticism had taught men to think. It was a light shining in a dark place. When Charlemagne decreed that every abbey in his realm should have a school he kindled the torches of knowledge throughout the land. And when the years passed on, and out of the schools arose the scholars, or schoolmen, learning and philosophy and the habit of thought revived. Scholasticism was imperfect. It did not strip away the night of the dark ages, but it penetrated its gloom. It did not destroy superstition, but it kindled a flame

---

[1] Bamp. Lec., 1885, p. 273.   [2] Hist. Interp., Farrar, p. 276.
[3] Ibid., p. 294.
[4] Ibid., p. 283; Hampden, Bamp. Lec., pp. 88–92.

that grew into the Renaissance and the Reformation, until the light was like the coming of the sun in its splendor.

Following scholasticism, and stirred into activity by its leaven, came the mental and spiritual forces which overthrew the despotism of church and empire. The feudal system was weakened; paper was invented, and the mariners' compass, and gunpowder, and the art of printing; the ocean was explored and continents discovered; and Copernicus, revelling in the stars, emblazoned the world with the shining truth of their systems.

And following the Renaissance came the Reformation; another thing not perfect, even as there are spots on the sun; but the most brilliant achievement of modern history, the pledge and guaranty of spiritual liberty for future generations. The Reformation was not the final development of doctrine. It was not a personality, invested with supreme authority in matters of faith and worship. It has not closed the cycles of Christian thought. But it broke the power of the great historic superstition. It bound the papacy to a narrower dominion, and disabled it forever. For the tide of history does not set again into the currents of the past. An effete heresy can never be completely rehabilitated. An ancient peculiarity can never anachronize the future and again become the prime characteristic of organic Christianity.

The Reformation raised its illustrious revolt against the authority of the Roman hierarchy. The voice of the pope had been the final answer to questions controverted. The people, craving certainty about eternal issues, had found it in the papal decrees. But when they threw off their allegiance to the pope certainty was gone, unless another infallible authority was found. Where could it be but in the Bible? Hence the famous saying of an English theologian: "The Bible, and the Bible only, is the religion of Protestants." That sentiment had sprung up in the hearts of many—in France, Germany, Switzerland, England—before it was coined into those famous words. Hitherto the Bible was thought to be inspired because such was the universal tradition. Jews and Christians, rabbis and fathers, bishops and schoolmen, had believed it to be inspired. Now there was an exigency demanding inspiration. With past authority stripped away, the Bible was the only refuge. It must be the voice of God. It must have been delivered by the Holy Ghost. At this time, also, the revival of learning had made it plain that the allegorical interpretation was untenable. It could not explain discrepancies and answer questions by lifting them above the vulgar letter into the serene, ineffable heaven of the mystical sense. And as allegory and the pope went hand in hand down into the darkness of an innocent disuse, the inspired Bible, in a more rational and human sense, simply answering the bombardment of interrogation, became the supreme dictator to the Protestant multitudes.

Luther, the most powerful personality among reformers, the man who gave the German people the German Bible, referring to the composition of the Scriptures, says: "The Holy Ghost is the all-simplest writer that is in heaven or earth." [1] Again, he says that "one letter, yea a single tittle of the Scriptures, is of more or greater consequence than heaven or earth." [2]

Calvin, the founder of modern Presbyterian theology, "like all the Reformers, speaks incessantly of the supreme and final authority of the Scriptures," and seems to have "held that Scripture flowed from the very mouth of God." [3] "When Réné, Duchess of Ferrara, daughter of Louis XII., had in a letter made the wise remark that David's example in hating his enemies was not applicable to us, Calvin curtly and sternly answered that 'such a gloss would upset all Scripture'; that even in his hatred David is an example to us and a type of Christ, and 'should we presume to set up ourselves as superior to Christ in sweetness and humanity?'" [4]

---

[1] Answer to Emser (see Köstlin, Luther's Theol., ii., 284).
[2] Luther on Heb. ii. 13; Gal. iv. 22.
[3] Hist. Interp., Farrar, p. 349; Calvin, Instit., i., 7, §5.
[4] Hist. Interp., p. 350.

It came to be common for the writers of the sacred books to be spoken of as "amanuenses of God," "hands of God," "scribes and notaries of the Holy Spirit," "secretaries, pens, reeds, harps, flutes, writing-tablets." The Bible was spoken of as "a divine effluence," "a part of God." One writer sedately argued the question whether the Scripture could be called a *creature*, and concluded that it could not. So complete was the indwelling of the Spirit in the Scriptures that a wicked person, if orthodox, was said to be illuminated by the reading of them *ex opere operato*. Quenstedt, Hollaz, Calov, and the Wittenberg faculty, in 1638, decreed that to speak of barbarisms and solecisms in the Greek of the New Testament would be a *blasphemy* against the writers and the Holy Ghost. Hebraisms in the New Testament were the desire of the Holy Spirit to make the style of the New Testament like that of the Old. Hellenistic Greek was Holy Greek, a form of speech peculiar to God. The *Formula Consensus Helvetica* declared that the very vowel-points and accents of the Hebrew Bible were all inspired. The Holy Spirit was said to have abdicated his agency to the written Word. "It is impious and profane audacity," said Calovius, "to change a single point in the Word of God, and to substitute a smooth breathing for a rough or a rough for a smooth."[1]

That such ideas as these—the main sentiment of lofty reverence for the Bible as of divine authority—found many an echo in the subsequent theology of the Continent, and of England and America, and have become the "popular" doctrine of the present day, is most certain. But that some of the reformers, as well as some of the rabbis, fathers, and schoolmen, expressed themselves at times in language that seems the very contradiction of their language elsewhere, is strangely true.

The *height* of doctrine on the subject of Inspiration is reached in the belief that not only the Hebrew text, but also the vowel-points and accents were inspired. The Hebrew

[1] Hist. Interp., pp. 374, 375.

language is one without vowels; it has only consonants. Vowel-points are inventions subsequent to the formation of the language. They were invented as substitutes for vowels, and used originally for the benefit of foreign students of that tongue. They are composed of certain dots and dashes, and combinations of them, and are placed, as the case may be, above, within, or under the consonants, and are used for *fixing* the text, so that there can be no variation in the translation. The letters *kl*, for example, might be written for *kol*, a voice, or for *kal*, a runner; *klh* for *kalăh*, to collect, or *kalah*, to burn. The vowel-points determine the word, establish the text. The work of placing the vowel-points and accents was done by a body of men known as the Masorites. The name comes from the Hebrew *masar*, which means "to deliver," and signifies the delivering or handing down of tradition. Thus the traditional reading of the Hebrew text of the Bible, the sound and meaning of the words, first transmitted from mouth to mouth by rabbi after rabbi, was finally thrown into lasting form by the placing of the vowel-points and accents; and the result is known as the Masora. But the vowel-points were not of Hebrew origin. The system of pointing the Shemitic languages is said to have begun in the Syrian school of Edessa, and was first used in the Syriac text of the Scriptures. From that it passed over first into the Arabic text and then into the Hebrew. The system was not invented complete, as we have it, but grew. It did not reach its present condition till the seventh century A.D., at Babylon, and the middle of the eighth century, in Palestine, and its full development was reached by successive steps that we cannot trace. It was invented a thousand years after the writing of the Hebrew Bible, and was applied to a Hebrew text "hardly later than the first Christian century."[1] Of this system it is a common opinion among the Jews that it came by divine reve-

---

[1] Biblical Study, C. A. Briggs, D.D., p. 152; and Professor W. Robertson Smith, Encyc. Brit., art. Hebrew, vol. xi., p. 600.

lation to the first member of the human family. "As to the origin and development of the vowels," says Azzariah de Rossi, a Jewish scholar, as quoted by Dr. Ginsberg, "their force and virtue were invented by, or communicated to, Adam in Paradise; transmitted to and by Moses; that they had been partially forgotten, and their pronunciation vitiated during the Babylonian captivity; that they had been restored by Ezra, but that they had been forgotten again in the wars and struggles during and after the destruction of the second temple; and that the Masorites, after the close of the Talmud, revised the system and permanently fixed the pronunciation by the contrivance of the present signs."[1] The theory of the inspiration of these points was maintained by such scholars as the Buxtorffs, Heidegger, Turretine, Voetius, and Owen, as well as by the Zurich Consensus.[2]

6. So far the stream of opinion was practically unbroken, and of one tendency. There were slight divergencies here and there in the nature of back-water and estuaries. Now and again a gust of enthusiasm would strike the surface of the stream in spots and lift the water in a spray as fine as the vowel-points and accents, attenuated and dampening as the mist that gathers in the shadows of the evening. And the waters were generally muddy. Christian opinion thought that somehow the book came from God, and struggled to show the manner of its coming and the nature of its divinity. It was not content to leave these matters where eternal Providence had left them. For man is vastly more particular than God. The one thing for which he longs, in doctrine, is definition. He would drive the abounding and pervading truth of God into an acute angle. He would trace it with a line of geometric straightness, and indicate it with the point of a needle, and settle it everlastingly upon a punctuation period. So, by individuals, the historic opinions about Inspiration have

---

[1] Biblical Study, Briggs, p. 141; De Rossi, The Light of the Eyes, iii., 59, 1574-75; Ginsberg, Life of Levita, in Levitas Massoreth, p. 53.
[2] Biblical Study, Briggs, p. 156; Hist. Interp., Farrar, p. 388.

been reduced to definitions and adorned with technical names. They have given us the *mechanical* theory, by which the writers were mere machines—passive instruments; "pens," and God wrote; "lyres," and God touched the strings and evoked the harmony. The *verbal* theory, by which the writers were not authors, but "amanuenses." God dictated, and they wrote; and every word and syllable became divine. The *dynamical* theory, which declares that the divine *power* wrought in the soul of the sacred author. The human faculties were all alive and energetic, but God lifted the soul into His own atmosphere. It saw His thoughts, and gathered His feelings, and made a record of them in the book. The *plenary* theory, which makes the inspired person "incapable of uttering or communicating any error with the inspired message." The *inductive* or *critical* theory, or theory of *selection*, which are practically one, and which affirm that the Scripture writers were inspired at times, and on occasion, to teach the eternal truths of God necessary to the soul's salvation and "instruction in righteousness." They have all had their advocates, zealous and enthusiastic, and have all proved more or less unsatisfactory to the remainder of Christendom. The voices of men are evidently not superior to the voice of God, nor to His silence. They cannot prevail, even with their fellows. And so the definitions have been various, and changing opinion has changed them and invented newer phraseology. At this particular point in history their number has been reduced and the outlook simplified. Modern scholarship has fused into one the definitions of the past, and given it the title of the *traditional* theory, while holding to the term *inductive* for its own. The traditional theory, broadly speaking, may be said to be "that the Bible as a whole and in all its parts is the Word of God, and as such endowed with all the perfections of that Word."[1] It is that which has *grown up*, as it were, out of the ages, until now. It never had a formal birth, and its majority was never announced; and yet it is here among

---

[1] Inspiration, Sanday, p. 392.

us, and has been everywhere in Christendom. The inductive theory has taken form within the last half-century, among the representatives of the latest biblical study and criticism. It is held by the leading scholars of the age. It has been spreading rapidly in popular belief, and it threatens to become the one great theory of the future.

And these are the two great contestants engaged in mortal combat upon the field of modern controversy. On either side the colors are flung to the breeze, the trumpets have sounded, and the heralds cry aloud.

Professor Gaussen says: "The Scriptures are given and guaranteed by God even in their very language. They contain no error; they say all that they ought to say, and only what they ought to say." Dean Burgon says: "The Bible is none other than the voice of Him that sitteth on the throne. Every book of it, every chapter of it, every verse of it, every word of it, every syllable of it, every letter of it, is the direct utterance of the Most High—supreme, absolute, faultless, unerring."[1] Dr. Charles Hodge says: "Protestants hold that the Scriptures . . . are the Word of God, written under the inspiration of God the Holy Ghost, and are therefore infallible, and consequently free from all error, whether of doctrine, of fact, or of precept."[2] Again: "All the books of Scripture are equally inspired. All alike are infallible in what they teach."[3] But, on the other hand, Tholuck says that this doctrine of Scripture being infallible, not only in its *religious*, but in its *entire* contents, and also in its *form*, arose not earlier than the seventeenth century.[4] Professor Sanday speaks, in effect, of how God "selected" one particular stock of mankind to receive a clearer revelation, and out of that stock "selected" individuals, and then "selected" times in which and subjects on which to *move* "their hearts and minds . . .

---

[1] How God Inspired the Bible, Smyth, p. 108.
[2] Theology, Hodge, vol. i., p. 152.
[3] Ibid., p. 163.
[4] Doctrine of Inspiration, Tholuck, Jour. Sac. Lit., vi., 331–369.

in a manner more penetrating and more effective than their fellows, with the result that their written words convey to us truth about the nature of God and his dealings with man which other writings do not convey with equal fulness, power, and purity. We say that *this special moving is due to the action upon those hearts and minds of the Holy Spirit.* And we call that action Inspiration."[1] Archdeacon Farrar says:[2] "Inspiration . . . does not imply an exclusive *theopneustia* * for the sacred writers," but "meant the influence of the Holy Spirit of God revealing himself in every great thought and utterance of the soul of man; given in the bestowal of 'every good and perfect gift.'"

Thirty centuries of opinion, and no conclusion! Nineteen centuries of Christian thought, and yet no dogma! Jew and Christian in all these ages uniting in the main idea, believing in the fact of Inspiration, yet never agreeing on a definition of its nature. Surely the individual of to-day may be pardoned if he is not wise above the Universal Church of God in the whole period of its life.

---

[1] Inspiration, Sanday, p. 127 (italics mine).
[2] Hist. Interp., p. 370.
* This Greek word means an in-breathing-of-God.

III.

HIS CRITICS.

> " For what am I ?
> What profits me my name
> Of greatest knight ? "

BUT out of the natural human faculty; out of the reason which is divine; out of the toil and patience and skill and learning of centuries; out of scholasticism and the Renaissance and the Reformation; under the benign providence of God, the great search-light of investigation has been turned upon the question of Inspiration. Near to the city of God, in the great harbor of rising and ebbing tides, among the shifting currents and the whirling eddies of speculation, stands the colossal figure of the Higher Criticism, as "Liberty, enlightening the world."

The Bartholdi Statue in New York harbor is not, of course, the source of the universal light, nor is liberty itself the one light of the world. But the colossus sends forth a flood of illumination over the dark waters of the bay, and criticism sheds its penetrating rays into the realms of biblical study.

Criticism means judgment, discrimination. In a literary sense it is an estimate of the complete value of a book. In dealing with the Bible it has two planes of action clearly marked. The lower plane, intellectually speaking, is that of the Hebrew and Greek text. The Lower Criticism, therefore, deals with that. It compares manuscripts, traces their history, seeks to ascertain what is the very language, what are the very words, originally written in the Scriptures. It strives after the absolute purity of the text. The higher plane of judgment or discrimination is that of the origin, literary forms, and contents of the Bible. The Higher Criticism, therefore, deals with the individual writings and groups of writings. It seeks to ascertain the authorship of the various books or parts of books, the times when they were written, the historical settings or circumstances, and the purpose of the writings, their relation to other writings of their groups, and to the whole collection. The Higher Criticism investigates the Bible as any other book might be investigated, and seeks to discover the value of each and all its utterances. It inquires whether the Bible is true in its history, science, geography, chronology. It takes all attainable testimony, external and internal —the testimony of profane history and that of the writings themselves. It studies their language, literary style and form, drift of thought, and handling of matters of secular learning and observation.

It is popularly supposed that the Higher Criticism is a "new thing under the sun." And while this is true as to its recent prominence and power, it is true only so far. Critical thought has had its representatives from time to time, at least since the second century before the Christian era. Acute thinkers and scholars have ever found food for question about the infallibility of the Bible in all its contents.

1. Aristobulus, the Alexandrian philosopher, the inventor of the allegorical method of interpretation, was the first to take away from the divinity of the letter. He was the first to start "the great religious problem—the discovery, if possible, of a test by which we may discern what are the eternal and irrepealable truths of the Bible, what the imaginative vesture, the framework, in which those truths are set forth in the Hebrew and even in the Christian Scriptures."[1]

2. The rabbins, without critical intent, followed in his footsteps. With all their worship of words and letters, they frequently set them aside for the sake of the mystical sense. They practised evasions of the law. For example, the law

Milman's Annals of St. Paul's, p. 467.

said: "At the end of every seventh year . . . every creditor that lendeth unto his neighbor shall release it."[1] Hillel nullified it by allowing the creditor a written contract by which he might claim the debt at any future time. Hillel "did it," says the Talmud, "for the good order of the world."[2]

3. Very strangely, but very clearly, the Septuagint bears testimony in the same line. It was to the Jewish people largely, and to the Christian fathers altogether, what King James's version is to us—a translation of the Bible in the popular tongue, in constant and general use. Yet it differs immensely, in words, passages, and entire books, from the Hebrew Bible. If, in the general estimation, the text of the Hebrew was literally divine, this tremendous divergence could never have been allowed.

And the New Testament adds a weightier testimony. It quotes the Old Testament repeatedly, but often in a marvellously liberal way. Not words, but sentiments, seem to be its object. If the words were inspired they only could have given the sentiment. It seems to say that while the thought was divine the language was human.

Moreover, the Messianic idea is the most conspicuous feature of the Hebrew Scriptures, and yet Hillel, one of the very greatest of Jewish doctors, "declared that no such Messiah would ever come;"[3] and Joseph Albo, a mediæval theologian, denies that the doctrine of the Messiah is a Jewish dogma.[4] They could not have valued the very text.

Besides this, the Talmud was made practically greater than the Bible, the rabbins higher authority than Moses, as Christ testified: "Ye made the commandment of God of none effect by your tradition,"[5] "teaching for doctrines the commandments of men;"[6] "and many such like things do ye."[7] "The voice of the Rabbi is as the voice of God," said the Scribes. "He who only studies the Scriptures is but an empty cistern."

---

[1] Deut. xv. 1, 2.   [2] Hist. Interp., Farrar, p. 64.
[3] Sanhedrin, f. 96, 2.   [4] Hist. Interp., p. 67.
[5] Matt. xv. 6.   [6] Mark vii. 7.   [7] Mark vii. 13.

"Words of Scribes," said Rabbi Johanan, "are akin to words of the Law, and more beloved."[1] How could it have been so if Moses and the Bible were thought to be inspired above all others?

4. The Christian fathers, with all their lustre of piety and fame, were often highly critical, in spite of their burning words of homage for the Scriptures. Canon Farrar says, of verbal dictation, that few if any of them "had any clear and fixed conception of the subject." Tholuck says that the ancient church held the *language* of the Bible to be human, and ascribed to it "contradictions in words and facts."[2] Farrar says that in Justin Martyr, Irenæus, Tertullian, Origen, Jerome, Chrysostom, and Augustine many passages "freely admit the human element," and "even attribute immorality and impropriety to many passages taken literally."[3] Justin, while believing in verbal dictation, "quotes the Sibyl and Hystaspes as genuine books." Tertullian thought that the apostles sometimes spoke only for themselves, as St. Paul, who said, "To the rest speak I, not the Lord." Origen thought the drunkenness of Noah, the incest of Lot, the rape of Tamar repulsively unprofitable reading; the law against eating vultures absurd. He said that there were enough discrepancies in the Gospels "to make one dizzy." Jerome thinks St. Mark, in chapter ii., verse 26, wrote Abiathar in mistake for Abimelech; the chronology of the Bible hopeless; St. Paul guilty of barbarisms, trivialities, poor proofs, bad taste, emotional passion. Chrysostom says: "Do not ask how these Old Testament precepts can be good now, when the need for them is past. . . . Their highest praise is that we now see them to be defective." Basil, speaking of the precepts of the law, says: "We pass from these to wisdom hidden in mystery."[4]

---

[1] Quoted by Farrar, pp. 62, 63.
[2] Bamp. Lec., Farrar, p. 264.
[3] Ibid., pp. 230, 172.
[4] See How God Inspired the Bible, pp. 75 ff.; and Hist. Interp., pp. 230 ff.

5. Among the schoolmen the difficulties that confronted the critical judgment were met by a theory of direct and indirect Inspiration. The direct was ascribed to those parts of the Bible which deal with doctrine. The passages which deal with history, chronology, or any matter of profane learning, were considered as indirectly inspired. Abelard said: "It is acknowledged that even prophets and apostles were not wholly free from error,"[1] and pointed out various discrepancies in the Gospels. Erigena said: "Let no authority terrify you from conclusions which the reasonable persuasion of right contemplation teaches."[2] Nicholas of Lyra insists upon the value of grammar, and care for the purity of manuscripts.[3]

Erasmus, in the early part of the sixteenth century, is said to be the chief founder of modern textual and biblical criticism. He denied the inspiration of the Book of Revelation. He was one of the first to declare the spuriousness of the passage in I. John v. 7, about the three heavenly witnesses. He denied infallibility anywhere but in Christ, saying: "Christ alone is called the Truth. He alone was free from all error." Luther, the apostle of the German Reformation, was abundantly free in criticisms. He rejected the Epistle of James, and denied the inspiration of the Epistle of Jude and the Book of Revelation. He said that the contents of the Bible had in them "wood, hay, stubble"; distinguished between the "Scriptures" and the "Word of God"; denied that Solomon wrote the Song of Songs or Ecclesiastes; showed the arrangement of the Book of Jeremiah to be unchronological; and made a variety of other criticisms. Denck said: "I esteem the Holy Scriptures above all human treasures; but not so highly as the Word of God, . . . written without pen or paper." Calvin points out the quotation in Matthew xxvii. 9, as from Jeremiah, as a mistake, and calls attention to other inaccuracies; says that the "seed of the woman," in Genesis iii. 15, meant originally "posterity," not Christ. He antici-

---

[1] Sic et Non, Prol. [2] De Div. Nat., i., 66.
[3] Bamp. Lec., 1885, pp. 274, 275.

pated modern criticism by interpreting the Messianic prophecies as referring primarily to events of their own days, and says that the idea that God made a throne of the mercy-seat was a "crass figment," deceiving even David and Hezekiah. Richard Hooker pleads against "attributing to Scripture more than it can have." Richard Baxter, on the same subject, says: "It is the devil's last method to undo by overdoing, and so to destroy the authority of the apostles by overmagnifying."

6. In 1679 Spinoza, the philosopher, published his "Tractatus Theologico-Politicus," in which he attacked the Mosaic authorship of the Pentateuch. It showed, he said, marks of a later date than Moses. As to names of places, Dan, so called in Genesis, was not then called Dan, but Laish.[1] The history was continued beyond the days of Moses. Mention is made in Exodus of stoppage of manna, which in Joshua is said to have stopped after the entrance into Canaan.[2] The expression in Genesis xxxvi. 31, "before there reigned any king over the children of Israel," implies that the writer lived after the establishment of the monarchy. Spinoza thought that Moses taught the elders, and that they wrote the commandments; that later they were collected and ascribed to suitable periods in Moses' life; that the present form of the Pentateuch was due to Ezra. Richard Simon, a Roman Catholic, a contemporary of Spinoza, thought that the laws of the Pentateuch were by Moses, and the history by the public scribe; and that Genesis was composed of earlier documents.

A deeper study and a keener critical insight were shown, in 1753, by Jean Astruc, a Roman Catholic layman, doctor and professor of medicine in the Royal College at Paris, and court physician to Louis XIV. He discovered marked traces of two separate documents in the Book of Genesis. Two accounts of the creation and two of the flood were among the indications. The documents were clearly stamped with the literary signs of different authorship; as, for example, one

---

[1] Gen. xiv. 14; Judg. xviii. 29.
[2] Ex. xvi. 35; Josh. v. 12.

speaks of God as Elohim, the other calls him Jehovah. Astruc supposed that Moses, in his composition, used the earlier documents. This theory, adopted by others, was called the "documentary hypothesis." Eichhorn, in 1780, combined the various results of previous critical effort into one common method, and first labelled it with the title of "Higher Criticism."

Vater and Hartmann, in 1815 and 1818, went further, and supposed the Pentateuch composed of a number of fragments "loosely strung together." Laws made in the time of David and Solomon were scattered through Deuteronomy. The other parts, written at various times, were collected into the present form sometime between the reign of Josiah and the Babylonish exile. This was called the "fragmentary hypothesis."

These, it is said, were both superseded by the "supplementary hypothesis," which sees two documents in the Pentateuch—the Elohist being the older, and the Jehovist, the later, using the Elohist document by adding to, commenting upon, and sometimes incorporating in his own work. It was adopted, with various modifications, by De Wette, Bleek, Stähelin, Tuch, Lengerke, Hupfeld, Knobel, Bunsen, Kurtz, Delitzsch, Schultz, Vaihinger, and others.[1]

De Wette sees marks of the two documents not only in Genesis, but in the first four books. Lengerke puts the Elohist in the period of Solomon and the Jehovist in that of Hezekiah. Tuch puts the first under Saul and the other under Solomon. Stähelin gives the Jehovist to the time of Saul and the Elohist to that of Judges. Hupfeld finds three authors—an earlier and later Elohist, and the Jehovist. Delitzsch thinks that Moses wrote the Book of the Covenant (Ex. xix.–xxiv.) and Deuteronomy, and the remainder was written by Eleazar the priest, Joshua, and the elders.

Ewald discovers seven different authors in the Pentateuch

---

[1] See Bishop Perowne's article, Pentateuch, in Smith's Bible Dictionary.

and Book of Joshua. In his view the oldest of the parts consists of a few fragments from the Book of the Wars of Jehovah; next, parts of a biography of Moses; then the Book of the Covenant, written in the time of Samson; the Book of Origines, by a priest in Solomon's time; the work of the third historian, or first prophetic narrator of primitive days, a person in the northern kingdom in the time of Elijah or Joel; the work of the fourth historian, or second prophetic narrator, about 800 or 750 B.C.; the work of the fifth historian, or third prophetic narrator, who lived shortly after Joel, and who collected the writings of his predecessors into one body of Scripture.

In 1818 Horne, in England, issued his "Introduction to the Critical Study and Knowledge of the Holy Scriptures," which embraced a study of the results of foreign criticism. In 1840 Coleridge's "Confessions of an Inquiring Spirit" appeared, with scriptural instances against the traditional doctrine of Inspiration. In 1862 Colenso, the English Bishop of Natal, startled the world by publishing an attack on the *historical* character of the Pentateuch and Book of Joshua, endeavoring to show that the parts which gave the most numerous details were the parts most difficult to believe. About the same time there was published a series of papers by "Eminent Englishmen," under the title of "Essays and Reviews," which breathed the spirit of the Higher Criticism.

Since that time the study of critical problems has immensely spread in the continental countries of Europe, in England and America. The exponents and adherents of the Higher Criticism are constantly growing more numerous. They claim the brotherhood of Tillotson, Warburton, Whately, Thirlwall, Heber, Alford, Arnold, and Kingsley, of Stanley and Maurice. And some of the most striking results out of all ages of investigation and of more than two centuries of criticism are to be found in the works of Kuenen among the Dutch, Wellhausen in Germany, and Canon Driver, of the University of Oxford.

IV.

HIS BLEMISHES.

"Out with it boldly: truth loves open dealing."
"And, where the offence is, let the great axe fall."

THE critics would say that the Higher Criticism has come forth "as a giant refreshed with wine," and put the traditional doctrine of Inspiration in bonds. Under the similitude of a man, the head is high above all bondage in the everlasting sunlight, and the heart is throbbing with the boundless liberty of God. But some of the insignificant portions of the body feel restraint. The critics would say that the Bible stands, like man, made, as it were, "in the image of God;" but it is a "broken image." They would say that it stands, again, in the likeness of that colossal figure in the prophet's vision whose head and body were of gold and silver, but the feet were made of clay.

The Higher Criticism has really dispelled something of the obscurity of past ages, and taken away somewhat of the veil to human sight, and made men see the Bible largely as it is, in plain and patent fact; and made them tremble, as Eli trembled, for the safety of the ark of God. But the Higher Criticism is not the synonym of infidelity. It has not overthrown the citadel of the faith. It has figured as the champion of clear knowledge and clear thought in the realms of fact and theology. It has been, indeed, a discriminating power. It has pointed out and emphasized the difference between inspiration and revelation and inspiration and infallibility. A revelation is the teaching of a truth beyond the reach of unassisted human reason—a truth unknown before. It may be made to the uninspired, as Christ revealed the essential spirituality of God to the adulterous woman of Samaria. Infallibility is the flawless accuracy, say, of a man or book. But inspiration, in a Christian sense, is the impulse and animation of a soul to speak or write as God would have it do. In human theology it has special reference to uttering prophecy and writing Scripture. It may come without the accompaniment of a revelation, while the prophet speaks or writes, in passionate enthusiasm, of the eternal truth which hath ever spoken to the common heart of man. It may come in company with fallibility, because it may not embrace the whole man, or the whole life, or the entire book, or every field of knowledge, divine and human. It is the confounding of these three which has confused the thought of Christendom for all these centuries, and turned King Liber into an idol. It is in the clarifying of the three that the Higher Criticism has won our gratitude. If, in the process, we have been robbed of cherished superstitions and fond errors, we need not, therefore, tremble for the faith: the edifice is not destroyed by the blotting out of inartistic frescoes. And then the Higher Criticism is not a god—or devil. We need not be transported with consuming fear. The Higher Criticism is a poor, imperfect creature, as all things human and mundane are. It has its own spots and blemishes, and it has made its own mistakes. It has *stumbled* upon truth; and then, again, with serene and open eyes, it has accepted falsehood and proclaimed it as invincible. The circle of its vision is incomplete, and so it has shifted its positions, and changed conclusions, and revised its articles of fact again and again. But still it is in large measure the fruit of that divine intelligence which is a part of the inheritance of the sons of God. And so it has brought "hidden mysteries" of human knowledge to light; it has laid bare much of the truth of history; and it has marshalled an array of arguments which stand in bristling opposition to that infallibility which Scripture never claimed for all its parts, and which never was a genuine element of inspiration. Let us look at something of the array:

1. *The Bible contains statements which scarcely call for so tremendous an endowment as infallibility.* St. Paul says to Philemon:[1] "But withal prepare me also a lodging;" to Timothy:[2] "The cloak which I left at Troas with Carpus, when thou comest, bring with thee." Such sayings do not even call for inspiration.

2. *The writers claim to speak, at times, for themselves alone, distinguishing God's sayings.* St. Paul says: "Unto the married I command, yet not I, but the Lord, Let not the wife depart from her husband. . . . But to the rest speak I, not the Lord."[3] One of the prophets[4] laments and exhorts because "a man's enemies are they of his own household," and adds, "Therefore I will look unto the Lord;" and then he turns and speaks *to* the Lord, saying, "Thou wilt perform the truth to Jacob, and the mercy to Abraham." So the prophets, in all their dialogues with God, mark the difference between God's speech and their own. They distinguish, also, between times when God was with them and when He was not. "The Word of the Lord came to Ezekiel" implies a time when He had not come. Elisha says, "The Lord hid it from me,"[5] signifying that God had not inspired him at that time. And St. Paul describes a like condition: "And now, behold, I go bound in the spirit unto Jerusalem, not knowing the things that shall befall me there."[6] So it would appear that the writers were not *always* inspired, and that the divine Being did not dictate everything they wrote.

3. *There are human elements in the Bible: Observation:* Ezekiel chooses for symbols the man and lion and bull and eagle which he saw on the Assyrian monuments and buildings. John, in the Apocalypse, uses figures familiar in his day as signifying political overturnings: "The sun shall be darkened,

---

[1] Philem. 22.
[2] II. Tim. iv. 13.
[3] I. Cor. vii. 10, 12.
[4] Micah vii. 6, 7, 20.
[5] II. Kings iv. 27.
[6] Acts xx. 22.

and the moon shall not give her light, and the stars shall fall from heaven." The burning of Rome was before his mental vision, the persecution of Nero, the confusions and errors of "the decade past." He saw in Nero or the Roman empire the beast; in the ten chief provinces the ten horns; in the seven emperors, Augustus, Tiberius, Caligula, Claudius, Nero, Galba, and Otho, the seven heads of the beast. *Style:* The personality of the author is stamped upon the various books. The literary manner is peculiar to the writer. The Fourth Gospel bears the impress of John; shows the profound insight of one who "leaned on Jesus' breast." The Epistles of Paul exhibit his own fiery zeal and tortuous logic, his digressions from one thought to another, led off by the suggestions of a word. Matthew is different from Mark, and Hebrews from Revelation; Jeremiah is far from Moses, and Ezra from Isaiah. *Imagination:* Which wings its flight from earth to heaven, and clothes the unseen in the brilliant earthly metaphors of jewels; stars; seas; fountains and rivers; mountains and hills; armies and their array; the battle and the siege; the dragon and beast, lion and eagle; the rainbow and the morning star. *Passion:* The psalmist says: "Break their teeth, O God, in their mouths;" "Blessed be he that taketh thy children and dasheth them against the stones;" "Let his children be fatherless, and his wife a widow. Let his children be vagabonds, and beg their bread." St. Paul turned upon the high priest with a burst of wrath, exclaiming, "God shall smite thee, thou whited wall." The same apostle "dubbed the whole race" of Cretans "evil beasts and liars"; and he passionately tells the Galatians, of certain who troubled them, "For I would they were cut off," which means the most cruel and barbarous of all mutilations. The process of composition seems to be perfectly natural, with the use of the common faculties of the mind.

4. *There are mistakes in the Bible, literal, verbal, and numerical.* If not mistakes, they would be contradictions. They are due, doubtless, to the carelessness or inaptitude of copy-

ists.* Of the famine sent upon David we read in one place "three years' famine,"¹ in another "seven,"² the Hebrew letter Gimel (G) standing for three, and Zayin (Z) standing for seven. The letters are very much alike. The Septuagint in both places has three. The number of "Solomon's officers that bare rule over the people" is given in one place³ as 250, in another⁴ as 550. This is owing to the mistake of changing the letters Resh Nun (R N) to Daleth Nun (D N). In one passage⁵ the age of Ahaziah when he began to reign is given as 22—Kaph Kaph (K K); in another⁶ as 42—Mem Kaph (M K). There are various other errors of this kind.

Of the various "readings"—which are differences of letters, words, phrases, texts—one writer⁷ estimates 800,000; another writer⁸ gives about 160,000. Robert Stephens says that he discovered 2384 in the oldest manuscripts of the New Testament alone. Of the three oldest manuscripts of the Greek Bible in existence, the Vatican, Sinai, and Alexandrian, Professor Westcott says of the differences: "There cannot be less than 120,000." Many of these, however, are mere matters of spelling and isolated aberrations of scribes. "Probably there

---

* The Bible was written on manuscripts. These were multiplied by copying. The copyists were clerks or scribes. They would sometimes mistake one letter for another very much like it. Seeing a word at the end of a sentence, it might chance that the same word ended a subsequent sentence, and turning the eye back to the manuscript the writer would go on from the latter of the two sentences, thus making an omission. In the early manuscripts all the words on a line were written without any space between them, and copyists made mistakes in dividing the words. Perhaps there were mistakes of memory, the scribe taking a sentence into his mind and in putting it down on the copy slightly changing the order of the words, or substituting some word of his own, as clerks frequently do to-day. Sometimes brief explanatory notes, or paraphrases, were put on the margin, and future copyists would put them into the text.

[1] I. Chron. xxi. 12.
[2] II. Sam. xxiv. 13.
[3] II. Chron. viii. 10.
[4] I. Kings ix. 23.
[5] II. Kings viii. 26.
[6] II. Chron. xxii. 2.
[7] Old Test. Canon, Dr. Moses Stuart, p. 169.
[8] Who Wrote the Bible? Dr. W. Gladden, p. 333.

are not more than from 1600 to 2000 places in which the true reading is a matter of uncertainty. The doubtful readings, by which the sense is affected, are very much fewer, and those of dogmatic importance can be easily numbered."[1]*

5. *The Bible misquotes itself.* St. Mark[2] quotes, as "written in Isaiah the prophet,"[3] the words, "Behold, I send my messenger before thy face, which shall prepare thy way before thee." The passage is not in Isaiah—though immediately following is a quotation from him—but in Malachi.[4] St. Matthew says: "Then was fulfilled that which was spoken by Jeremy the prophet, saying, And they took the thirty pieces of silver, the price of Him that was valued, whom they of the children of Israel did value; and gave them for the potter's field, as the Lord appointed me."[5] This is not in Jeremiah at all; it is, substantially, in Zechariah, but with very different wording. Jerome said that he had heard of and seen an apocryphal writing of Jeremiah in which the words quoted occur.[6] Such lapses are not consistent with the verbal inspiration of quotation.

6. *The apostles of Christ differed among themselves* about the bearing of the Jewish law upon Christians. At that time one

---

[1] Quoted by Dr. Gladden, pp. 345, 346.

* There are wide differences of a more serious nature in the various manuscripts—differences in whole collections of manuscripts. The Septuagint contains several entire books which are not in the Hebrew Bible at all. They form the bulk of what we now call the Apocrypha: such as Tobit and Judith, the Wisdom of Solomon and Sirach, Baruch and Susanna, and Bel and the Dragon. And the apocryphal books are not separated to themselves, but are mingled indiscriminately among the other books. In the Septuagint the Books of Daniel, Esther, and Jeremiah have additional matter not found in the Hebrew text. And there are considerable differences between the two texts in the Books of Samuel and Kings.

[2] Mark i. 2.

[3] The words "in Isaiah" are not in King James's version, but are in the Greek.

[4] Mal. iii. 1.   [5] Matt. xxvii. 9, 10; Zech. xi. 12, 13.

[6] Com. in Ev. Matt. ad loc., ed. Migne, vii., 213.

of them, at least, could not have been infallible. St. Paul says that Peter and James and John were in error, and that Peter and others were guilty of "dissimulation": "But when Peter was come to Antioch, I withstood him to the face, because he was to be blamed. For before that certain came from James, he did eat with the Gentiles: but when they were come, he withdrew and separated himself, fearing them which were of the circumcision. And the other Jews dissembled likewise with him; insomuch that Barnabas also was carried away with their dissimulation. But when I saw that they walked not uprightly according to the truth of the gospel, I said unto Peter before them all, If thou, being a Jew, livest after the manner of Gentiles, and not as do the Jews, why compellest thou the Gentiles to live as do the Jews?"[1] This is a powerful attack upon the inspiration of St. Peter at that time.

7. *One—or more—of the apostles was mistaken about the second advent.* St. Paul thought that Christ would come again in his day. He even thought that in this conviction he spoke by direct counsel of Christ: "For this we say unto you by the word of the Lord, that we which are alive and remain unto the coming of the Lord shall not prevent them which are asleep."[2]* St. John writes, in the name of his Master, "Surely I come quickly," and answers, in devout anticipation and prayer, "Amen. Even so, come, Lord Jesus."[3] St. James says, "The coming of the Lord draweth nigh."[4] St. Peter says, "The end of all things is at hand."[5]

8. *There are errors of chronology in the Bible.* The Bible limits the reign of King Ahab to 918–897 B.C.; the Assyrian

---

[1] Gal. ii. 11–14.   [2] I. Thess. iv. 15.

* Of this Bishop Ellicott says: "It does not seem improper to admit that in their ignorance of the day of the Lord the apostles might have imagined that He who was coming would come speedily."[1] Conybeare and Howson say: "The early church, and even the apostles themselves, expected their Lord to come again in that very generation."[2]

[3] Rev. xxii. 20.   [4] James v. 8.   [5] I. Pet. iv. 7.

[1] Com. in loc.   [2] Life and Ep. of St. Paul, i., 401.

monuments affirm that Ahab was engaged in a battle at Qarqara B.C. 853, forty-four years after his supposed death. In the Bible Jehu's reign ends in 856; by the monuments he pays tribute to Assyria in 841—a difference of fifteen years. In the Bible the reign of Azariah of Judah ends in 751; by the monuments he is defeated by Tiglath-Pileser in 737. In the one Menahem pays tribute to Pul about 770; by the other in 737. In the one Damascus fell in 740; by the other in 732. Pekah is said to have reigned twenty years; by the Assyrian inscriptions it could have been no more than seven years. The Bible gives the campaign of Sennacherib in Judah as in the fourteenth year of the reign of Hezekiah; the monuments put it in the twenty-fourth. The Jewish historian seems to have confounded the invasion of Sennacherib with that of Sargon, ten years earlier.[1]

9. *There are historical mistakes in the Bible.* The second book of Kings[2] implies that Sennacherib conquered Hamath, Arpad, Sepharvaim, and Samaria, whereas the monuments record that this was done by Sargon. So is called in the Bible "king of Egypt," whereas he was only the commander of the Egyptian army. Pul and "Tiglath-Pilneser" are described in Chronicles[3] as two different persons, whereas they were one and the same.

In the Book of Daniel Belshazzar is called the "last king of the Chaldeans"; there is an account of the siege of Babylon; the king is said to have been slain; and Belshazzar is said to be the son of Nebuchadrezzar. The monuments testify that Nabonidos was the last king, and that Belshazzar never reigned at all; that Nabonidos, the last king, was not slain; that there was no siege of Babylon, but that Cyrus entered the city in peace; and that Belshazzar was the son of Nabonidos, and not of Nebuchadrezzar.

In the same Book of Daniel Darius is called the son of Ahasuerus, who in profane history is known as Xerxes, whereas

---

[1] See The Higher Criticism and the Monuments, Sayce, pp. 408 ff.
[2] II. Kings xviii. 34.   [3] I. Chron. v. 26.

the Assyrian inscriptions state that Darius Hystaspis was the *father* of Xerxes. The name Belteshazzar, resembling one which means, in Babylonian, "O Beltis, defend the king," is corrupted in Daniel, the first syllable being changed so that it means "he caused to live," making the combination, "He caused to live—defend the king," which is a meaningless compound, and unknown in Babylonian.[1] Abed-Nego is a similar corruption, probably substituted for Abed-Nebo, "servant of Nebo."

10. *The Bible contradicts itself.* The account of the creation given in the first chapter of Genesis has the following order: vegetation, animals, man; that in the second chapter is: man, vegetation, animals, woman. In the accounts of the flood, in the sixth chapter it is said: "Of every living thing of all flesh, two of every kind shalt thou bring into the ark;" in the seventh chapter: "Of every clean beast thou shalt take to thee seven and seven." In Genesis xxi. 31 it is said that Abraham called a well Beer-sheba because of a covenant between him and Abimelech; but in Genesis xxvi. 33 the name Beer-sheba is said to have originated with Isaac, nearly a century later than the other incident, and on account of an oath between Abimelech and him. In chapter xx. Abraham passes off Sarah as his sister, lest Abimelech should kill him to take her; but in chapter xxvi. it is Isaac that has passed off Rebecca as his sister before Abimelech. Leviticus[2] directs the release of the Hebrew slave in the year of jubilee, the fiftieth; Deuteronomy[3] in the seventh year. In Numbers[4] the firstlings of oxen and sheep are given to the priest; in Deuteronomy[5] to the owner, who should eat them at the sanctuary. The law of Moses forbids the offering of sacrifices anywhere but at the main sanctuary—the tabernacle or the temple; but "Samuel sacrifices on many high places, Saul builds altars, David and his son Solomon permit the worship at the high places to continue, and the historian recognizes this as

---

[1] See High. Crit. and Mon., p. 532.
[2] Lev. xxv. 40.   [3] Deut. xv. 12.
[4] Num. xviii. 18.   [5] Deut. xii. 7.

legitimate because the temple was not yet built.[1] In northern Israel this state of things was never changed. The high places were an established feature in the kingdom of Ephraim, and Elijah himself declares that the destruction of the altars of Jehovah—all illegitimate according to the Pentateuch—is a breach of Jehovah's covenant."[2] The Levitical law forbade any one but the high priest entering the "holy of holies"; yet Samuel slept "in the temple of the Lord, where the ark of the Lord was."

In the second book of Samuel[3] it is said that Absalom rebelled against his father "forty years," after his return to Jerusalem, though the history of David's reign shows that it could not have been for more than one or two years.

In the Book of Judges[4] the taking of Debir by Caleb is said to have been "after the death of Joshua"; in the Book of Joshua[5] it is described as occurring during Joshua's life.

In the second book of Kings[6] Hoshea is said to have begun to reign in Israel "in the twentieth year of Jotham," king of Judah; three verses later it is said that Jotham reigned only "sixteen years."

The second book of Samuel[7] says that David took from Hadadezer, king of Zobah, "a thousand and seven hundred horsemen;" in I. Chronicles[8] we are told that he took "a thousand chariots, and seven thousand horsemen." In Samuel[9] David's census shows 800,000 warriors of Israel and 500,000 of Judah; in Chronicles[10] 1,100,000 of Israel and 470,000 of Judah. In Samuel[11] David pays Araunah for his threshing-floor "fifty shekels of silver," about thirty dollars; in Chronicles[12] "six hundred shekels of gold," about thirty-four hundred dollars. In the second book of Chronicles[13] it is said

---

[1] I. Kings iii. 2–4.
[2] Old Test. in Jew. Ch., Professor W. R. Smith, pp. 220, 221.
[3] II. Sam. xv. 7. [4] Judg. i. 1, 11, 12. [5] Josh. xv. 15–19.
[6] II. Kings xv. 30, 33. [7] II. Sam. viii. 4. [8] I. Chron. xviii. 4.
[9] II. Sam. xxiv. 9. [10] I. Chron. xxi. 5. [11] II. Sam. xxiv. 24.
[12] I. Chron. xxi. 25. [13] II. Chron. xv. 19.

that from the fifteenth to the thirty-fifth year of Asa's reign "there was no war"; in the first book of Kings [1] that "there was war between Asa and Baasha king of Israel all their days." In the second book of Samuel [2] it is said: "The anger of the Lord was kindled against Israel, and He moved David against them, saying, Go, number Israel and Judah;" in Chronicles: [3] "And Satan stood up against Israel, and moved David to number Israel;" and it is added that because of this numbering "the Lord sent pestilence upon Israel: and there fell of Israel seventy thousand men." [4]

St. Matthew [5] says that Judas "brought again the thirty pieces of silver to the chief priests and scribes," and "cast down the pieces of silver in the temple," and "went and hanged himself"; and "the chief priests took the silver pieces" and "bought with them the potter's field." St. Luke, in the Book of Acts, [6] says that "this man"—Judas, not the chief priests—"purchased a field with the reward of iniquity"—the silver pieces; and, not that he hanged himself, but that, "falling headlong, he burst asunder in the midst, and all his bowels gushed out."

11. *There are seeming discrepancies in the Bible.* The genealogy in St. Matthew from David to Christ gives twenty-eight generations, and makes Jacob appear as the father of Joseph; the one in St. Luke gives thirty-eight generations, and names Heli as the father of Joseph. SS. Matthew and Mark tell of the healing of the blind near Jericho. They say it was as Jesus left the city; St. Luke tells of such an incident as he was going to the city. St. Matthew says that there were two blind men healed; SS. Mark and Luke mention only one. SS. Matthew and Mark record the healing of Peter's wife's mother before the calling of the apostles, St. Luke after the calling. SS. Matthew and Mark tell of one angel at the sepulchre of Jesus; SS. Luke and John tell of two. St. Matthew says that Jesus was crucified at nine o'clock, "the sixth hour;" St. John

---

[1] I. Kings xv. 32.　　[2] II. Sam. xxiv. 1.　　[3] I. Chron. xxi. 1.
[4] I. Chron. xxi. 14.　　[5] Matt. xxvii. 3-8.　　[6] Acts i. 16-19.

says at twelve, "the ninth hour." The inscription on the cross is given by the four Evangelists in four different forms: "This is Jesus the King of the Jews;" "The King of the Jews;" "This is the King of the Jews;" "Jesus of Nazareth the King of the Jews."

With some scholars these discrepancies are reconciled, upon various theories; to others they appear irreconcilable.

The scientific difficulties about the Bible have not been given in this account, because to this writer the great difficulties do not seem to exist. It is inconceivable that any writer of the literary capacity displayed by the author, or authors, of the Book of Genesis, should design or attempt to make a scientific statement on such stupendous subjects as the origin of the universe, of man, or of evil, in such microscopic space. On these subjects the language is sufficiently broad and rhetorical to permit its application to almost any scientific theory. It cannot, therefore, be in conflict with, say, a "nebular theory" or ascertained "evolution." Any philosophy may open its statements with the preface that "the earth was without form, and void"; and any science which sees the human body mouldered into dust may say that man was formed from "the dust of the ground." In the account of the flood, also, the language is not technical, but epic, and the phrases which set forth the idea that all flesh and all mankind were destroyed, and that the waters covered the whole earth, are like those which say that David's kingdom or Solomon's shall be established "forever," or that there were in Jerusalem, at Pentecost, men "from every nation under heaven." The language is rhetorical, popular, and thus interpreted by those who spoke and heard it. Like it is the famous poetical quotation in Joshua:

> "Sun stand still in Gibeon,
> And moon in the valley of Ajalon;
> And the sun stood still,
> And the moon stood,
> Until the people avenged themselves on their enemies."

The poets do not write for the "schools."

Perhaps the most deeply serious hindrance to belief in the traditional idea of the Bible is in the fact that God is not seen and does not speak. All representations to the contrary are born of the poverty of human thought and the feebleness of human language. They are metaphors, figures of speech, clothing the divine Being in the likeness of feeble men. Echoing the universal testimony of the Scriptures, the first of the Thirty-nine Articles states that God is "without body, parts, or passions." Jesus Christ said, "God is spirit." To say that He spake to Moses "face to face" is to use a piece of rhetoric. It is recorded that Moses specially pleaded for a glimpse of the august Countenance, and was denied it.[1] It is also stated in that connection that Moses did catch a glimpse of His "back parts," whatever that may mean. But St. John, in his Gospel, declares that "no man hath seen God at any time";[2] and St. Paul speaks of Him as "the King eternal, immortal, invisible,"[3] "dwelling in the light which no man can approach unto; whom no man hath seen, nor can see."[4]

[1] Ex. xxxiii. 23.
[2] John i. 18.
[3] I. Tim. i. 17.
[4] I. Tim. vi. 16.

V.

HIS LIMITATIONS.

"They that stand high have many blasts to shake them."

THERE are further difficulties in the way of the infallibility of the Bible, growing out of its methods of composition, custody, and authorship.

The word "Bible" is not to be found in the book itself; it does not so call itself. The Jews called the writings of prophets and historians the "Scriptures" or "Sacred Scriptures" —that is, "writings" or "sacred writings." The early Christians called them "The Books." This was the habit among Christians till the eighth century. In the thirteenth century the whole collection was generally called "The Book."

Greek Christians, in the early days, used the terms "Old Covenant" and "New Covenant" to describe the books respectively of the old and new dispensations. The word "testament" is derived from one of the words used by the Saviour at the institution of the Supper: "This is my blood of the new testament." In Hebrew the word is *b'rith;* in Greek, *diatheke;* in Latin, *testamentum.* It is from this last that our word "testament" comes. The word was used by some of the fathers, and its use was fixed, for modern times, by Luther when he put upon his German translation of the Bible the titles "Old Testament" and "New Testament."

Among the early Jews the Bible was divided into lessons from the Law and from the Prophets. Among Christians Ammonius of Alexandria divided the Gospels into short chapters. In the fifth century other divisions were made—the chapters in the Book of Acts and the Catholic Epistles by Euthalius of Alexandria. The present chapters were arranged by Cardinal Hugo, of St. Carus, in the thirteenth century. The present arrangement of verses was made by Robert Stephens, in an edition issued in 1551.

The Hebrew Scriptures were written with iron pens, with ink made of lampblack dissolved in gall-juice, and on skins from animals. The skins were cut in strips, which were joined end to end and rolled from opposite extremities on two sticks, making a scroll. Scrolls of the ancient pattern may be seen in modern Jewish synagogues. The skins, of course, were highly durable, but in the lapse of centuries the original manuscripts of all the Scripture books have disappeared. The manuscript from which our English Bible descended seems to have been cut or torn, at the end of the second book of Chronicles, right in the middle of a sentence, where there should have been no pause at all, not even enough to be punctuated with a comma. The first part of the sentence is repeated, and the conclusion added, in the third verse of the first chapter of the Book of Ezra; in fact, Ezra begins with the twenty-second verse of the last chapter of II. Chronicles.

It is said that we have no Hebrew manuscript of the Old Testament older than A.D. 1100, and that the oldest are full of clerical mistakes.[1]

The books of the New Testament were doubtless written originally on papyrus—a common writing-material of that day —composed of the fibre of the papyrus plant, with some glutinous substance, subjected to pressure.

There are versions of the Old Testament which antedate all manuscripts in existence—the Septuagint, the Chaldee and Samaritan Targums, the Syriac Peshitto, and the Vulgate. The three oldest manuscripts in existence are known as the Vatican, Sinai, and Alexandrian MSS. These Bibles are written in Greek, with only uncial, which are capital, letters. Of other uncial manuscripts there are, if we include fragments,

[1] Bamp. Lec., 1885, p. 388, note 4.

fifty-six of the Gospels, fourteen of the Acts, six of the Catholic Epistles, fifteen of the Pauline Epistles, and five of the Apocalypse. Of the cursive manuscripts—cursive means "running hand," in which letters were joined as we join them now, written not in capitals, but small letters—there are about two thousand of the books and various parts of the New Testament. The uncial letters show a more ancient custom of writing than the cursive.

The Vatican and Sinai Bibles are supposed by scholars to have been written in the fourth century, the Alexandrian in the fifth. The Vatican seems to be the oldest of the three. It is so named because it was found in the Vatican Library at Rome in the year 1475. It contains the Septuagint translation of the Old Testament and the books of the New Testament—except the last five chapters of Hebrews—the two Epistles to Timothy, those to Titus and Philemon, and the Apocalypse. It contains also the Apocrypha. The Sinai Bible was found by Constantine Tischendorf in a convent at the foot of Mount Sinai: a few leaves in 1844; nothing in 1853, when he returned to find that the monks had hidden them from him; and the entire book as it now is in 1859, when he returned armed with a letter from the Czar of Russia, the head of the Greek Church. It is now in St. Petersburg. It contains twenty-two books of the Old Testament, the New Testament, the "Epistle of Barnabas," and a part of the "Shepherd of Hermas." The Alexandrian Bible was brought by Cyril Lucar, Patriarch of Constantinople, from Alexandria in Egypt, and by him presented to Charles I. of England, who kept it in his private library. In 1753 it was taken to the British Museum, in London, where it remains. It contains the following books, in the following order: Vol. I.: Pentateuch, Joshua, Judges, Ruth, the two books of Samuel, Kings, Chronicles; Vol. II.: the twelve minor prophets, Isaiah, Jeremiah, Baruch, Lamentations, the Epistle of Jeremiah, Ezekiel, Daniel, Esther, Tobit, Judith, I. Esdras, II. Esdras (which includes Nehemiah and part of Ezra), and the four books of the Maccabees; Vol. III.: an Epistle of Athanasius to Marcellenus on the Psalms, the Hypothesis of Eusebius on the Psalms, the Book of Psalms (containing one hundred and fifty-one psalms and fifteen hymns), Job, Proverbs, Ecclesiastes, Canticles, Wisdom of Solomon, Ecclesiasticus; Vol. IV.: the four Gospels, Acts, Epistle of James, First and Second of Peter, three of John, Jude, fourteen of Paul (including Hebrews), Revelation, two Epistles of Clement to the Corinthians, and eight psalms of Solomon.

1. *Manuscripts were few in number, and exposed to a thousand and one mischances*, from ignorance, carelessness, controversies, political dissensions, fire, earthquake, confusions incident upon epidemics, war, captivity, the destruction of cities and kingdoms.

During the reign of Josiah in Judah, six or seven centuries after Moses, "a book of the law of the Lord by Moses" was found by Hilkiah the priest. Whatever that book was it was clearly lost, or unknown, at least for some considerable period before that time. In another instance King Jehoiakim seizes a manuscript of Jeremiah's prophecy, cuts it in strips with a penknife, and burns it in the fire.

2. *Hebrew writings were generally anonymous.* The names of the authors were not affixed; authorship of books was a matter of tradition. Look into your English Bible, into the various books; not at the titles, which are modern, but into the text itself. It does not say who wrote the books. "The vision of Isaiah the son of Amoz," begins one. "The words of Jeremiah the son of Hilkiah," reads another. It is not said that either Isaiah or Jeremiah *wrote* these books. The prophets were the clergy of their time—the great preachers. The scribes were another class. There is nothing to *prove* the authorship of the books of the Pentateuch, Joshua, Judges, Samuel, Kings, Chronicles, Ezra, Nehemiah, Esther, Job, Jonah, Ruth, many psalms, Lamentations, and Hebrews. It has been argued by many eminent scholars of high Christian faith that Daniel could not have written the book called by

his name, because the book is not in the Hebrew collection of the prophets. Neither he nor his book is mentioned in the contemporaneous histories of the Exile. Jesus, the son of Sirach, B.C. 200, gives a list of the prophets and other great men of Israel, but Daniel's name is not among them. Daniel is in Babylon, yet he says nothing of the return from exile and the rebuilding of the temple, so soon to follow—matters that absorbed Jewish thought and longing. Persian words and Greek words in the prophecy strongly argue for a later authorship than the day of Daniel. The author seems to have lived in the days of the Maccabees, and to have put his words in Daniel's mouth. Modern scholars are generally agreed that chapters xl.–lxvi. of Isaiah are by some "great unknown." Tradition has assigned these books to persons popularly supposed to have written them; but only tradition. If the infinite and eternal Being had designed that their authorship should be a matter of grave consequence to the world surely He would have taken some precaution to assure us of it.

3. *The titles of many books were not given by the writers.* It is not known that any of them were. With Jews and Christians the titles have been different. The Jews frequently called books by the first word or two in them. So it was in the Pentateuch: Genesis was called *B'reshith*, "In the beginning;" Exodus was *Y'elleh Sh'moth*, "Now these are the names;" Leviticus was *Vayyikra*, "And he called." They called the Book of Psalms *Th'hillim*, which means, literally, praise-songs, or, liberally, praise-book or hymnal. The titles to many of the single psalms were given by editors or compilers. Jerome gave the Books of Chronicles their present name. The Jews called them "Events of the Times"; the Septuagint names them "Paraleipomena," which means "things left over," or supplements. The present title of the Epistle to the Hebrews is not in some of the earliest manuscripts. We have it, "The Epistle of Paul the Apostle to the Hebrews;" the original title was, "To the Hebrews." In the title to the Epistle to the Ephesians the word "Ephesians" is not in the

Sinai or Vatican manuscripts. The place is left blank, as though several copies had been intended, and the space was to have been filled with the name of the particular church to which the copy should be sent.

4. *Methods used for stirring to inspiration were sometimes human and carnal.* Natural instruments were used to stimulate natural excitement and credulity. Music was made a prominent and potent factor. Saul meets "a company of prophets . . . with a psaltery, and a tabret, and a pipe, and a harp," "and the Spirit of God came upon him, and he prophesied."[1] Again, when he was seeking David, and had sent messengers after him to Ramah, and afterward followed them himself, both the messengers and Saul caught the enthusiasm of the "company of the prophets," and "the Spirit of God was upon them" also, and they also "prophesied."[2] When Elisha was called upon by the kings of Israel, Judah, and Edom, to deliver them in their war with Mesha, king of Moab, before he would deign to notice his supplicants he cried, "Bring me now a minstrel."[3] "And it came to pass, when the minstrel played, that the hand of the Lord came upon him."

Dreams also were favorite instruments for laying open the hearts of men to receive the divine knowledge; as in the cases of Abimelech and Jacob, Joseph, Gideon, and Samuel. Then there were trance and ecstasy, as in the case of Balaam, "falling into a trance, but having his eyes open."

Oracles also were consulted, that men might see, by the oracular aid, hidden truth. The children of Dan consulted Micah with his "ephod" and "teraphim," that they might find a territory for a possession, and Micah said, "Go in peace: before the Lord is your way wherein ye go."[4] And David, seeking knowledge whether Saul would pursue him to Keilah, and the men of Keilah deliver him to Saul, calls to Abiathar the priest, "Bring hither the ephod."

---

[1] I. Sam. x. 5, 10.
[2] I. Sam. xix. 20–24.
[3] II. Kings iii. 15.
[4] Judg. xviii. 3–6.

The methods of attaining to prophecy even became matters of training and education, as witness the "schools of the prophets," where, also, companionship and sympathy might kindle prophetic enthusiasm.

5. *The divine communications were not recorded until long after they were given*, and then often not by the prophets themselves. The divine promises to Abraham, the dreams of Jacob and Joseph, the dreams of Joseph the reputed father of Jesus, the message of the angel of the Annunciation to the Virgin Mother, are instances. The first group of these were popularly supposed to have been written by Moses, generations after Abraham, when his family had become a nation; the others were written down, not by Joseph and Mary, but by Matthew and Luke years afterward. "The narrative of the events which happened at Sinai is some centuries later than those events."[1] And the records we have of the sayings of the Lord Jesus Himself were not written by apostles and evangelists till long after "a cloud received Him out of their sight."

6. *Prophecy uses the tenses of verbs with marvellous freedom.* It sweeps from century to century and back again, intermingling the ages with strange facility, if God put every word into every prophet's mouth. Isaiah, centuries before, says of Christ, centuries after, "Unto us a child *is* born, unto us a son *is* given." Zechariah, in a single chapter—the ninth—gazes upon the martial figure of Alexander the Great, then upon the gentle form of Jesus Christ, and then "suddenly reverts to the age of the Maccabees," three hundred years before. Jeremiah[2] pictures the capture of Babylon by Cyrus and its final destruction as one event, although they were centuries apart.

7. *The Bible writers drew from other sources.* They gathered materials as other authors do. If Moses wrote the Pentateuch he incorporated in it some things of which there were previous accounts. The archæologists tell us that Ramses II. was the Pharaoh of the Oppression, and that he died in 1281 B.C.;[3]

---

[1] Sanday, Bamp. Lec., 1893, p. 234.   [2] Jer. l. li.
[3] High. Crit. and Mon., Sayce, pp. 241, 242.

that the Exodus took place in the reign of his son and successor, Meneptah II.[1] This would bring the time of Moses not later than the latter half of the thirteenth century B.C. The Tel-el-Amarna tablets, discovered in Egypt in 1887, date from the century before the Exodus. They show that Babylonian culture had spread through Palestine and Syria into Egypt. They are written in the Babylonian language, and show that that language was familiar to the cultured classes of those countries, just as French has been familiar in the countries of modern Europe. Poems of the creation, stories of the Garden of Eden, of the fall of man, of the flood, of the tower of Babel, which the archæologists tell us date from over two thousand years before Christ, and which were current in Babylonia and Assyria, as the monuments show, were therefore familiar, it is said, to cultured people in Moses' time. Moses was, the Bible tells us, "learned in all the wisdom of the Egyptians." The Egyptians were "wise" in the language of the Babylonians, and, it seems fair to infer, knew their cosmology and religion. If, therefore, Moses wrote the first chapters of Genesis, it seems fair to infer that he drew *something* of his story from the traditions, beliefs, and historical accounts current in his day.

The almost universal conviction of modern scholars is that Genesis is composed, in part, of earlier documents. Indeed, the biblical authors refer to other documents by name, in some instances quote from them, and at least show that they were consulted. There are: the "Book of the Wars of Jehovah;"[2] the "Book of Jasher,"[3] in which is the "Song of the Bow"; the "History of Samuel the Seer,"[4] the "History of Nathan the Prophet," and the "History of Gad the Seer"; the "Prophecy of Ahijah the Shilonite," and the "Visions of Iddo the Seer";[5] the "Book of Shemaiah the Prophet";[6] the "Book of the Chronicles of the Kings of Israel"[7] and the

---

[1] High. Crit. and Mon., Sayce, p. 240. [2] Num. xxi. 14.
[3] II. Sam. i. 18. [4] I. Chron. xxix. 29. [5] II. Chron. ix. 29.
[6] II. Chron. xii. 15. [7] I. Kings xiv. 19.

"Book of the Chronicles of the Kings of Judah,"[1] which are not *our* "Kings" and "Chronicles"; the "Acts of Uzziah";[2] and the "Book of Jehu the Son of Hanani."[3]

8. *Some laws and institutions are prior to Moses*, although he has been thought the first of the sacred writers. Sacrifice was common among all nations. Circumcision, the Bible itself shows, was practised by the Arabs, Moabites, Ammonites, and Edomites. Herodotos says that it was used by the Phenicians, Colchians, and Ethiopians. From earliest history it was practised by the Egyptians, and still is; and inscriptions indicate it in Babylonia.[4] The word "Sabbath" is of Babylonian origin, from *Sabattu*,[5] which is described on the Babylonian tablets as "a day of rest for the soul." The Assyrians derived the word "from two Sumerian or pre-Semitic words, *sa* and *bat*, which meant, respectively, 'heart' and 'ceasing.'" In Babylonia even the king "must not eat flesh cooked over the coals or in smoke, . . . change the garments of his body," offer "sacrifices," wear "white robes," or ride in a "chariot."

9. *There are successive authorships in the Old Testament.* Of this the great majority of the books bare traces. That God should inspire one man to write one infallible book is more comprehensible than that He should inspire many men to write many fragments, which somehow should be gotten together and thus constitute an infallible volume. It is generally regarded[6] as scarcely doubtful by the higher critics—among them the professors of Hebrew in the universities of Oxford, Cambridge, and Edinburgh—that the Pentateuch embraces four separate documents by four distinct authors, of marked individualities of literary style. Before them all, in point of antiquity, is the Song of Deborah, in the Book of Judges, which is regarded as the oldest piece of Hebrew literature in existence. The four documents of the Pentateuch are known

---

[1] I. Chron. ix. 1.   [2] II. Chron. xxvi. 22.   [3] II. Chron. xx. 34.
[4] High. Crit. and Mon., pp. 280, 281.   [5] Ibid., p. 74.
[6] Old Test. Criticism, Quarterly Rev., April, 1894.

as the Jehovist, which is reckoned to have been written at the end of the ninth or beginning of the eighth century B.C.; the Second Elohist, about fifty years later; the Deuteronomist, not later than 621 B.C.; the First Elohist, or Priest's Code, in the first quarter of the fifth century B.C. These four are generally admitted among scholars. Each existed as an independent code before incorporation into the Pentateuch. Each can be, in its main features, distinctly traced, and while there are some differences among critics as to details, there is practical unanimity as to the main outlines. In these documents there are three distinct codes of laws: (1) the Book of the Covenant, embracing chapters xx.–xxiv., xxxiv. of the Book of Exodus; (2) Deuteronomy, the popular and prophetic code; (3) the Priest's Code, of which Leviticus is the centre, with Exodus xxv.–xxxii., xxxv.–xl., and Numbers i.–x., xv.–xix., xxv.–xxxvi. The laws of the three codes, as we now have them, gathered in and scattered through the Pentateuch, "probably date from every period in the history of Israel;" some of them, like circumcision and the Sabbath, going back before Moses, and others belonging to the period between Ezekiel and Ezra, or perhaps later.

The oldest Pentateuchal document, be it observed, is credited to the eighth or ninth century B.C., whereas it is estimated that Moses flourished in the thirteenth.

Besides the four authors referred to, many of the critics have become convinced that each document received contributions from several other authors, and that there were various modifications by various editors, the entire combination and arrangement of the Pentateuch having been most probably made by Ezra about the year 444 B.C.

Evidences of the separate documents may be seen in the two accounts in Genesis of the creation and the flood, those of the creation giving in the first chapter one order and in the second chapter another order in which the universe was made. In the accounts of the flood, intermingled as they are in the sixth chapter, let us see one or two examples:

Jehovist: "And Jehovah saw that the wickedness of man was great in the earth."

Elohist: "And Elohim looked upon the earth, and, behold, it was corrupt; for all flesh had corrupted his way upon the earth."

Jehovist: "And Jehovah said, I will destroy man whom I have created from the face of the earth."

Elohist: "And Elohim said, . . . The end of all flesh is come before me ; . . . and, behold, I will destroy them with the earth."

Jehovist: "But Noah found grace in the eyes of Jehovah."

Elohist: "And Noah walked with Elohim."

And so with words, phrases, style peculiar to the writer, names, allusions to customs and events that are not such as the traditional author could refer to, through many books the impress of other authors and editors may be traced. "Even Deuteronomy," says one writer, is probably the work of a "school or succession of writers, who have left their impress deeply traced upon the Books of Joshua, Judges, Kings, and . . . Samuel." Isaiah is not all Isaiah, say others; Jeremiah has had other words mingled with his own; and neither is methodically or chronologically arranged. Jonah appears to have been written three or four centuries after his day, and contains "reminiscences" of the Psalms. Micah and Zechariah have other prophecies mingled with their own. Malachi may not be even a name, and is wholly unknown in person. The Psalms and Proverbs were touched by many hands. In Job the speeches of Elihu are interpolated, and mar the symmetry of the drama. Chronicles is a compilation from many sources; and Ezra and Nehemiah another compilation, by the same hands, long after their heroes had "fallen asleep."

VI.

HIS MINISTERS.

"Thou wilt not utter what thou dost not know."

WHAT, then, did Moses write? It is very difficult to answer, say the critics. "The older historical writing was all of it the work of prophets." There is "a double stream of narrative" in the Pentateuch, written during the periods of the Monarchy and the Exile, "variously dated between 900 and 750 B.C."

1. It is thought that the law grew up originally out of the decisions of Moses, for "Moses sat to judge the people."[1] He said,[2] "Because the people come unto me to inquire of God: when they have a matter, they come unto me; and I judge between one and another." But Jethro, his father-in-law, thought this too heavy a tax and strain upon him, and proposed that he should appoint others to relieve him of this labor and responsibility. "And Moses chose able men out of all Israel. . . . And they judged the people at all seasons."[3] And so, perhaps, a fuller law grew up out of their decisions and those of Deborah and Samuel.[4]

2. The Bible claims directly that Moses wrote some things; the Book of the Covenant;[5] and, on the second pair of tables, "the ten commandments"; and the story of the defeat of Amalek;[6] and "the words of the law" in a book.[7]

3. It does not seem probable, however, that Moses wrote the

---

[1] Ex. xviii. 13.   [2] Ex. xviii. 15, 16.   [3] Ex. xviii. 25, 26.
[4] Judg. iv. 4, 5; I. Sam. vii. 16, 17.   [5] Ex. xxiv. 4, 7.
[6] Ex. xvii. 14.   [7] Deut. xxxi. 24–26.

account of his own death in Deuteronomy; or that he wrote, "Moreover the man Moses was very great in the land of Egypt, in the sight of all the people;"[1] or, "Now the man Moses was very meek above all the men which were on the face of the earth;"[2] or, "There arose not a prophet since in Israel like unto Moses."[3]

The expression "the Canaanite was then in the land"[4] looks as though it were written by some one at a time when the Canaanite was not in the land, a period long after the death of Moses. The expression "while the children of Israel were in the wilderness"[5] looks like the writing of one who had got out of the wilderness, which Moses never did but by death. "These are the kings that reigned over the land of Edom before there reigned any king over the children of Israel."[6] Moses knew of no king. Saul was the first king, at least three hundred years after Moses. In the twentieth chapter of Numbers, in the first verse, it is recorded that the children of Israel reached Kadesh. This was in the first month of the third year of the wandering. Yet in the twenty-second verse of the same chapter there is a record of Aaron's death at Mount Hor, which was in the fortieth year of the wandering. Here is a chasm in the history of thirty-eight years. It does not look like a continuous history written by one hand, and that the hand of the central figure in the history. In Exodus, twenty-third and thirty-sixth chapters, there are two records of the same set of laws, repeated almost word for word; in Leviticus, eighteenth and twentieth chapters, a similar instance. One writer would scarcely have given the repetitions.

4. *It is important to observe* that neither the Pentateuch nor any of its separate books state that Moses was the author of them; that none of the later books of the Old Testament state it. They refer to Moses not as an author or writer, but as a leader, an intercessor, a prophet.[7] They also refer to the law

---

[1] Ex. xi. 3.   [2] Num. xii. 3.   [3] Deut. xxxiv. 10.
[4] Gen. xii. 6.   [5] Num. xv. 32.   [6] Gen. xxxvi. 31.
[7] Jer. xv. 1; Micah vi. 4; Hos. xii. 13.

of Moses, but never say that it was written by him. The apocryphal books of the Old Testament do not state it; nor the teachings of Christ; nor any apostolic or sub-apostolic writer; nor any council—ecumenical, national, or provincial; nor does any consensus of the Christian fathers, nor any one father, speaking with authority.

On the other hand, it is claimed in the Pentateuch that certain parts of it were written by Moses. This is recognized by the later books of the Old Testament. It became customary to speak of the whole as written by him. In the three centuries before Christ there grew up a widespread belief that he wrote the whole;[1] and this popular belief has been handed down to our own day.

5. The gathering together of the books of the Old Testament into what is known as the canon marked the estimate put upon them as of divine origin, and stamped them as "Scripture." How each separate document or book was regarded when written we have no means of knowing; at least some of them were not regarded as sacred from the beginning. It is generally agreed among scholars that the canon of the law was settled by Ezra in the year 444 B.C.* It is largely agreed, also, that the canon of the prophets was set-

---

[1] See Old Test. Crit., Quarterly Rev., April, 1894.

* Others of the present books were written before that time, and others afterward. The dates assigned to them by Professor Sanday in his Bampton Lectures, and Professor Driver in his Introduction, are as follows: Psalms, from David, 977, downward to the second century B.C.; Song of Songs, after Solomon, 937; Obadiah, perhaps 844; Joel, perhaps 817; Amos, 760; Hosea, 740; Isaiah, 737–700; Micah, 700, chapters vi., vii., 686; Zechariah, ix.–xiv., eighth century (Driver); Nahum, 624; Zephaniah, 621; Habakkuk, 608; Ruth, period of Exile, sixth century (Driver); Jeremiah, 627–580; Lamentations, perhaps 627–580; Job, not earlier than 627, perhaps in sixth century (Driver); substantial completion of Books of Kings, 600; Ezekiel, 592–572; Isaiah, xl.–lxvi., 546–538; Haggai, 520; Zechariah, i.–viii., 520–518; Malachi, shortly before 432 (Driver); Ecclesiastes and Esther, not earlier, perhaps later, than 332 (Driver); Ezra and Nehemiah, about 300; many psalms, final arrangement of the Book of Proverbs, perhaps Jonah, about this time; Chronicles, 300; Daniel, 164.

tled in the course of the third century B.C.[1] Nehemiah had gathered together the Books of Joshua, Judges, Samuel, and Kings, and about his time began the third collection, of such books as made up the Hagiographa. The process of making this collection extended through several centuries, and the sacred authority of some of the books was disputed till a late date. The fact that the Chronicles stand at the end of the Hebrew Bible indicates that they were admitted to the canon at a late date. The Books of Canticles and Ecclesiastes were long disputed among the Jews, and the question of their admission was not settled by any authority until the Jewish Synod of Jamnia, in A.D. 90, about sixty years after the death of Christ, when the canon of the Old Testament was finally closed; although even after this some devout Jews continued to be doubtful about the Book of Esther.

6. Of the history of the New Testament books much the same may be said as has been said of the Old Testament. The gospel was first oral, transmitted from mouth to mouth for years after it was first spoken by the Master. The titles of the books as we have them are not always correct, as in the Epistles to the Ephesians and Hebrews, before mentioned. The earliest of the books, the First Epistle to the Thessalonians, was not written till A.D. 52, some twenty years after the death of Christ. The Gospel of Luke was a little earlier than the Acts, which was written in 63. The Gospels of Matthew and Mark came a little later, apparently before 70. The Book of Revelation dates from 68 or 69, and the Gospel and Epistles of St. John somewhere in the nineties. Some of these books also appear to be anonymous. The authorship of Hebrews has never been settled; that of Jude and II. Peter has been questioned. Even so distinguished a theologian as Calvin denied that Peter had written the second epistle of his name, and so great a man as Luther denied that John had written the Apocalypse.

The New Testament does not consist of the first writings

---

[1] Bamp. Lec., 1893, p. 101.

ever made on the subject of Christ and the gospel. St. Luke says: "Forasmuch as many have taken in hand to set forth in order a declaration of those things which are most surely believed among us . . . it seemed good to me also . . . to write."[1] From this it appears that there were "many" accounts, notes, memoranda, from which the New Testament writers drew. They also compiled, as did the Old Testament writers. They also gathered materials, as historians have done before and since. They quote also from books not in the canon, although the quotations are of a liberal kind. St. James quotes from Sirach;[2] Romans and Hebrews from Wisdom;[3] Corinthians from Judith;[4] and Jude from Enoch.[5]

The original manuscripts of these books, written on papyrus, soon perished. Copies were multiplied, and marginal notes crept into the text, some of which we can easily distinguish by comparing King James's version with the Revised Version. Readings varied, and discrepancies arose.

The New Testament books were written in the Greek language, while the language spoken by Christ was Aramaic, so that we have only a very few of the actual words of Christ. In one instance He said, *Ephphatha*[6]—"Be opened;" in another, *Talitha cumi*[7]—"Damsel, I say unto thee, Arise;" in a third, *Eli, Eli, lama sabachthani?*[8]—"My God, my God, why hast thou forsaken me?" And these are all.

7. Some of the Old Testament books are quoted in the New, and as sacred Scriptures, which is thought to imply an indorsement of them as of divine authority. But, as we have seen, other books are also quoted. If quotation stamps Isaiah as divine it also stamps Enoch as divine. And non-quotation leaves the books not quoted without indorsement, which would mark invidiously Ecclesiastes, Canticles, Esther, Ezra, and

---

[1] Luke i. 1, 3.   [2] James i. 19; Sirach v. 11, iv. 29.
[3] Heb. i. 3; Wis. vii. 26; Rom. ix. 21; Wis. xv. 7.
[4] I. Cor. ii. 10, 11; Judith viii. 14.
[5] Jude 14, 15; Enoch, ch. ii.   [6] Mark vii. 34.
[7] Mark v. 41.   [8] Matt. xxvii. 46.

Nehemiah, which are not so much as in any way referred to in the New Testament.

It is true that Christ himself refers to the Old Testament, as in the case of Jonah: "As Jonah was three days and three nights in the whale's belly, so shall the Son of man be three days and three nights in the heart of the earth."[1] And it is thought that this stamps the narrative of Jonah as literal fact and indorses the inspiration of the book. But Christ also speaks of the rising and setting of the sun, which by parity of reason would set the divine seal to a false fact. The sun does not rise and set, but the current metaphors may well have been taken upon the divine lips; and the current estimate of Jonah may well have been used by the divine Teacher for purposes of illustration. If the story of Jonah was not true why did He not denounce it? It may as well be asked why, in speaking of the story of creation, He did not declare that the six days were not natural days of twenty-four hours. It is not profane to say that perhaps He did not know. He had submitted to limitations when He "emptied himself" of His glory and became man. There were things which He declared He did not know: "But of that day and that hour knoweth no man, no, not the angels which are in heaven, neither the Son, but the Father."[2] And St. Luke says:[3] "And Jesus increased in wisdom and stature, and in favor with God and man."

8. The canon of the New Testament was formed gradually, as was that of the Old. It was a process, not an act. The apostolic writings were read with respect. It does not appear that they were at first regarded as Scripture. As time passed they grew in value. They were nearer the origin of Christianity than others. They were written by men who knew the Lord Jesus. In the latter half of the second century they were gathered together for the first time. The first part was called "The Gospel," and contained the four Gospels; the second part was called "The Apostle," and contained the

---

[1] Matt. xii. 40.   [2] Mark xiii. 32.   [3] Luke ii. 52.

Acts, thirteen Epistles of St. Paul, one of St. Peter, one of St. John, and Revelation.

Numerous other Christian writings sprang up, and Christians began a process of sifting, to determine which should be regarded as Scripture. Fathers and churches were not at first agreed; they had various lists of books, which each regarded as sacred—some more so, some less so. The value of them was not equal in the eyes of fathers and churches. Origen (A.D. 185–253) seems to be the first to furnish a list of the books as we have them now, though he expresses doubts of II. Peter and II. and III. John. Athanasius (A.D. 363) is the next to give the complete canon. And the question of what should constitute the New Testament seems to have been finally settled at the Councils of Carthage, in 397 and 419.

VII.

HIS FRIENDS.

"As on a mountain-top the cedar shows,
That keeps his leaves in spite of any storm."

IS all this vague, irrelevant, inconclusive on the question of Inspiration? Is it *ad rem* as to the subject of Introduction, and *de aliis* as to Inspiration? It might seem so. If so it would be nothing worse than an imitation of the modern fashion in writing books. They deal profusely and exclusively with some other subject than the one to which their pages are dedicated. In this instance, however, there would be the generous excuse of necessity. For there is not a phase in the history of biblical opinion which is not of interest in the investigation; and there is not an item in the history of criticism which is not of consequence in the settlement of the issue.

If the books are divine, why all the natural processes in their origin and history? If God had settled their status, why the slow judgment of men and churches to pass upon it? Do they contradict themselves? Then they are not, so far, of God. Does Inspiration cover the book, or does it only here and there inflame its pages? Are there verbal mistakes? Then it cannot be verbally inspired. Is the history false in certain details? Then that portion cannot be inspired. Are the writers passionate and contentious? Then in such moods the divine afflatus was wanting. Are they not always inspired? Then there must be discrimination about their sayings. Are the original manuscripts lost? Then we cannot tell, amid the sea of differences, the original words in every text. Was there an "apostolical succession" of writers in a single book? Were there innumerable copies? Were there compilations, extracts from profane history, editors and redactors? Then to make it all infallible there must have been infallibility all along the line. Is Inspiration of such a nature as to bridge over all such difficulties, or of such a nature as to stand supreme among them?

As to the quantity of "Inspiration" in these pages, there is so little to be had, in any work, on the direct question that the massing of that alone would scarcely make more than a generous leaflet. The entire literature about it is busily and voluminously occupied with something else. If the foregoing sketch is vague it is so because the whole original picture is vague, the outlines dim, the features blurred. The only thing sharply drawn and positive about it is here and there a sharp and very positive squint. The vagueness is historical. It stretches all along the line. It is the leading characteristic of the subject. The study of Inspiration is like a pursuit of the will-o'-the-wisp, a flickering and wandering light in the dank and swampy regions of controversy. The effort to grasp it is like an effort to grasp the subtle and universal ether. There is no authoritative theory about it in Catholic Christendom. The language that defines it is, and has ever been, purely personal and private. The definitions, like the persons who define, are all irresponsible to history and the universal conscience. The earlier ones are obsolete in the presence of modern learning. They have passed from the scientific view. The verbal, mechanical, plenary, and dynamical have been melted into one, which is called traditional, perhaps because it is such a deliciously indefinite term to apply to such a delicious cluster of confusions. The latest theory, the inductive, is only the speculation and the term of a coterie of theologians. However popular it may be, or may become, the gentlemen who conceived it have never received divine authority or ecclesiastical commission to fix it everlastingly upon the Church of God.

The word "inspiration" is itself vague, mystical, elusive. The great body of believers do not know its meaning, and cannot tell, *exactly*. The numerous theologians explain it in so great a variety of ways that the common mind is puzzled and mystified, and becomes guilty of the suspicion that even the theologians cannot tell, *exactly*. Moreover, *the word is not adjudicated*. Therefore no man is bound by the definition of another. And every man has a certain liberty to define it for himself, if he is hungry and thirsty for a definition. Stand solidly upon the *word*, and no human soul, or congregation of souls, has the right to force you from your strong foundation, or wring another syllable of confession from your lips. Indulge in wide, circuitous excursions of the mental faculties, or wander amid a wilderness of tangled romances, about its infinite suggestion, but all the while cling resolutely to the *word*, and you can never be convicted of heresy. Literally speaking, it means an inbreathing, from the Latin *in* and *spiro*, to breathe into. *Theopneustos*, the Greek adjective which St. Paul, in the famous passage in one of his Epistles to Timothy,[1] applied to Scripture, means inbreathed-of-God. It is from *Theos*, God, and *pneo*, to blow or breathe. To say "inspiration" in the Christian sense is an abbreviated way of saying inspiration-of-God. Inspiration in the Christian sense, therefore, is the blowing of the breath of God. And the man or the book which is inspired is the man or the book into which God has blown His breath. But God is not corporeal. He has no breath. He does not blow. The expressions are anthropomorphic and metaphorical. The word "inspiration" is a metaphor. And viewing its sober and its sombre history, one might echo the apposite irony of the farcical wit which said that "figures of speech are the pillars of the Church." Sagely and solemnly, without the flicker of a smile upon their beclouded faces, which might reveal some faint suspicion of the poor humor of their undertaking, for nineteen centuries, summoning all ancient and modern wisdom to aid them in their

---

[1] II. Tim. iii. 16.

task, men have been struggling to convert a metaphor into an exact theological term. If they have failed, is not the nature of their undertaking the clear and irresistible explanation of the failure ? A sketch of the history of Inspiration is inconclusive ! Yes, in the nature of the case, it *must* be so. The history itself is inconclusive. The *facts* are inconclusive. The striking and utter difficulty of conclusions, the widespread and radical differences in the long catalogue of opinions, the utter absence of any conclusion on the part of the Catholic Church of all ages, the deep silence of the Book of God itself, are the insuperable facts which stand in unbroken array along the whole vista of the centuries.

But the lack of definitions does not blind us to the essential truth. Behind, and overtowering and overshadowing the history of doctrine, the failures of human wisdom, the confusions of controversy, and the inaccuracies of a book, there is a power greater than all metaphor, which wins the wonder and allegiance of the soul. That was a happy faith, in ancient times, which made men feel that signal talents were the direct gift of God. That was a reverent belief among the heathen that the poet was inspired, the sculptor, the painter, the dashing general, the brilliant and victorious king. The genius came not by the slow course of nature, but by the swift supremacy and interposition of the Deity. In this faith the Jew and Gentile were united. But the Jew was ever "peculiar." In his belief it was not the secular, but the sacred faculty which came from God. Inspiration was *religious*. It was not the poet *per se*, nor the artist, who was inspired, but the prophet, or the priest, or the psalmist. When the prophet was seized with powerful religious feeling he believed he was inspired. When the feeling burst forth into words he believed that the inspiration had passed into his speech. When his soul was visited with a high thought he believed it came from God. Where else could it come from ? God spoke to him. Who else could have spoken thus divinely ? The prophet could not see that the lofty, spiritual visions of his soul sprang out of the dusty soil. He could not see that they were born of man in his degradation and sin. They *must* have come from God. There was no other source for such sublime ideas. God *must* have spoken, because the thoughts were turned to words, and such words were never human. And as the prophet warned and pleaded with the people, he poured forth the torrent of his own powerful conviction that God had spoken when he said, "Thus saith the Lord of hosts." There was within him a force not terrestrial. It came from the ineffable heights. It was a power for truth and righteousness with which God invested the prophets and The Book.

So, in the high simplicity of this thought, to turn to the evidences of Inspiration is a more grateful task than sketching the history of criticism.

1. *The universal conviction of prophets and writers that they were inspired* is one of the most striking and impressive lines of evidence. From Moses to John there is the same note, gathering strength along the centuries, until at last it has burst into a unison that fills the ages. Too often to be enumerated here are the cries, "Thus saith the Lord of hosts," "The word of the Lord came," "Hear ye the word of the Lord." And often it is apparently against the prophets' wills. They feel themselves impelled by a divine constraint. Moses urges that he is "slow of speech and of tongue." Isaiah cries, "Woe is me! for I am undone; because I am a man of unclean lips." Jeremiah exclaims, "Ah, Lord God! behold, I cannot speak; for I am a child." Ezekiel is warned that "briers and thorns" will be with him, and that he will "dwell among scorpions." Amos declares that he was "no prophet," neither "a prophet's son," but "a herdman, and a gatherer of sycamore fruit"; yet "the Lord took" him, and said, "Go, prophesy." They all have a consciousness that the "Spirit" is upon them, and that consciousness is accorded them by others: "The Lord said unto Moses, Write this for a memorial in a book;" "And Moses wrote their goings out according to their journeys by the commandment of the

Lord;" "This word came unto Jeremiah from the Lord, saying, Take thee a roll of a book, and write therein all the words that I have spoken unto thee." David says: "The Spirit of the Lord spake by me, and His word was in my tongue;" Micah says: "I am full of power by the Spirit of the Lord;" John says: "He saith unto me, These are the true sayings of God."

And <u>the inspiration of the prophets is abundantly granted in the New Testament.</u> Says St. Paul: "Well spake the Holy Ghost by Esaias the prophet." "Every Scripture inspired of God is profitable." Says the Epistle to the Hebrews: "God, who at sundry times and in divers manners spake in time past unto the fathers by the prophets." Again: "Wherefore as the Holy Ghost saith, . . . They shall not enter into my rest;" "The Holy Ghost this signifying;" "The Holy Ghost also is a witness to us." Christ himself said: "David himself said by the Holy Ghost." And thus is the New Testament replete with testimony to the Old, and the New Testament writers continually express the same consciousness of the Spirit in themselves and the Church as those of the Old. St. Luke, in Acts, says of Stephen: "They were not able to resist the wisdom and the spirit by which he spake." Agabus begins his prophecy with "Thus saith the Holy Ghost." The Apostolic Council says: "It seemed good to the Holy Ghost and to us." St. Peter says: "We are witnesses of these things, and so is also the Holy Ghost." Again: "Holy men of God spake as they were moved by the Holy Ghost." St. Paul says: "I have received of the Lord that which also I delivered unto you;" "Which things also we speak, not in the words which man's wisdom teacheth, but which the Holy Ghost teacheth;" "Unto the married I command, yet not I, but the Lord;" "I think also that I have the Spirit of God;" "If any man think himself to be a prophet, or spiritual, let him acknowledge that the things that I write unto you are the commandments of the Lord." St. John says that he was "in the Spirit." But supreme in their testimony are the promises and assurances of Jesus Christ: "It is not ye that speak, but the Spirit of your

Father which speaketh in you;" "I will pray the Father, and He shall give you another Comforter, that He may abide with you forever; even the Spirit of truth;" "When He, the Spirit of truth, is come, He will guide you into all truth: ... He will show you things to come. ... He shall take of mine, and shall show it unto you;" "Lo, I am with you alway, even unto the end of the world."

2. *The New Testament refers to the Old as though its prophecies could not fail, and points to their fulfilment.* It refers to the Old as having the highest authority. St. Matthew says: "Now all this was done, that it might be fulfilled which was spoken of the Lord by the prophet, saying, Behold, a virgin shall be with child, and shall bring forth a son." St. Luke says: "All the prophets from Samuel and them that followed after, as many as have spoken, they also told of these days." In like terms the prophets are mentioned in a multitude of instances. St. Luke in the Gospel [1] and in Acts, [2] St. Paul in II. Corinthians,[3] the apostles in council,[4] speak of Moses and the law as though the law was final; and Christ also speaks of the law [5] of Moses and the book [6] of Moses as of divine authority. SS. Philip,[7] Peter,[8] Stephen,[9] and Paul,[10] as also Christ [11] Himself, speak of Moses as a prophet who wrote of Christ. The divine Teacher repeatedly emphasizes the power and divinity of the Scriptures: "Ye do err, not knowing the Scriptures, nor the power of God;" "They are they which testify of Me;" "All things which are written in the law of Moses, and the prophets, and the psalms, concerning Me;" "This that is written must yet be accomplished in Me;" "Beginning from Moses and from all the prophets, He interpreted to them in all the Scriptures the things concerning Himself;" "Did ye never read in the Scriptures, The stone which the builders rejected, the same is become the head of the corner;" "This is he of

---

[1] Luke xxiv. 27. [2] Acts xxviii. 23. [3] II. Cor. iii. 15.
[4] Acts xv. 21.   [5] John vii. 23.   [6] Mark xii. 26.
[7] John i. 45.   [8] Acts iii. 22–24. [9] Acts vii. 37.
[10] Acts xxvi. 22. [11] John v. 46, 47.

whom it is written, Behold, I send My messenger before thy face, which shall prepare thy way before thee;" "The Scripture cannot be broken;" "Verily I say unto you, Till heaven and earth pass one jot or one tittle shall in no wise pass from the law, till all be fulfilled."

3. *The Scriptures prophesy, and the prophecies are fulfilled.* Long before there was any danger to the northern and southern kingdoms Isaiah prophesied their downfall. He tells how at first Jerusalem shall be threatened with an army, and the threat shall be removed: "Woe to Ariel, to Ariel, the city where David dwelt! . . . I will camp against thee round about, and will lay siege against thee with a mount, and I will raise forts against thee. And thou shalt be brought down, and shalt speak out of the ground. . . . Moreover the multitude of thy strangers shall be like small dust, and the multitude of the terrible ones as chaff that passeth away: yea, it shall be at an instant suddenly. . . . And the multitude of all the nations that fight against Ariel, even all that fight against her and her munition, and that distress her, shall be as a dream of a night vision."[1] The sequel, the fulfilment, is found in the history of Sennacherib: "Then the angel of the Lord went forth, and smote in the camp of the Assyrians a hundred and fourscore and five thousand. . . . So Sennacherib king of Assyria departed."[2] Again, the prophet predicts the captivity a hundred and fifty years, before it occurred: "Behold, the days come, that all . . . shall be carried to Babylon: nothing shall be left. . . . And . . . thy sons . . . shall they take away; and they shall be eunuchs in the palace of the king of Babylon."[3] Micah predicts the same disaster.[4] Nahum[5] foretold the destruction of Nineveh a hundred and fifteen years before the event. And of Tyre[6] it was foretold that she should be "a rock for the spreading of nets"; and that Israel[7] should be "scattered among the nations," and Jerusalem[8] "trodden

---

[1] Isa. xxix. 1-7. [2] Isa. xxxvii. 36, 37. [3] Isa. xxxix. 6, 7.
[4] Micah ii. 10. [5] Nahum, ii., iii. [6] Ezek. xxvi. 5.
[7] Zech. vii. 14. [8] Luke xxi. 24.

down by the Gentiles." "Who as I," saith the Lord, "declareth the thing that shall be?"

4. *The Scriptures contain most solemn warnings against the mutilation of their message.* It is true that such expressions were not framed after the entire body of the Scriptures were written and bound up together, but they seem to voice a sentiment which is applicable to the Scriptures as a whole: "What thing soever I command you, observe to do it: thou shalt not add thereto, nor diminish from it;"[1] "Every word of God is pure. . . . Add thou not unto His words, lest He reprove thee, and thou be found a liar;"[2] "I testify unto every man that heareth the words of the prophecy of this book,[3] If any man shall add unto them, God shall add unto him the plagues which are written in this book: and if any man shall take away from the words of the book of this prophecy, God shall take away his part from the tree of life, and out of the holy city, which are written in this book. He which testifieth these things saith, Yea: I come quickly."

And thus suddenly we are at the end of the evidence of Inspiration just as we enter its threshold. That Israel and Christendom have ever believed the Bible to be the Book of God, and that the Bible so thinks of itself, is the only direct testimony that we have of the fact of Inspiration. Whatever the miracles of past ages sealing the dealings and sayings of God with men; whatever of Burning Bush, or Dewy Fleece, or Pillar of Fire, or Shechinah of Glory, or Voice of Thunder, in the centuries gone; whatever pitiful yet august Power in the Redeemer's healing of the sick and raising of the dead; whatever the unspeakable might and transcendent mastery of the resurrection of Jesus the Most High God, the tide of time has left them in the region of distant history. The bar of temporal limitations has been stretched across them. The Book has come since. They never spoke directly of the Book. They stood in the realm of incident and event, and there they linger even for ever and ever. The Book is in the realm of

---

[1] Deut. xii. 32. [2] Prov. xxx. 5, 6. [3] Rev. xxii. 18-20.

literature. Jesus never said that the Old and New Testaments complete were inspired, dictated of God throughout their borders from leaf to cover. The skies were never opened and the proclamation issued. We cannot step back into the presence of the brilliant visions of the ancient saints; we cannot see them in their divine frenzies, and watch the movement of the heavenly pens, and trace the dumb vicissitudes of manuscripts. And therefore Inspiration is nowhere made an article of the faith. That such a thing exists and has existed through the stream of centuries is evident. But let us never blink at the truth. Let no fondness for phraseology ever intoxicate our reason and blind us to the verities. Let no fanatical fidelity make us insist on terms and definitions which are not explicitly revealed. Let us not, as theologians or as Christians, confuse or lead astray the millions of mankind, or impose upon their consciences a word of man. It were better to blot the word "inspiration" from theology and the dictionary. It has come, alas! to stand too often and too long for temporary or local or personal definitions. Every fanatic or zealot would foist his own opinions on the public and fain make them believe that *they* are Inspiration. The wisest define not. The greatest define not. So the divine Being Himself, which is enough. So the divine body—the Church—which overshadows while it embraces the individuals of the Catholic universe, "angels and living saints and dead." The Catholic creeds have never given us a definition—neither the decrees of the Council of Trent, nor the Articles of the Anglican Church, nor the formularies of the Lutheran communion. Inspiration is an atmosphere, not a technicalism. It is assumed, not stated; assumed because a patent fundamental to divine truth, and because of the awful and irresistible experience and witness of the spiritual faculties of man in every age of human history. Thus undefined, the Prayer-book mentions it: "The *inspiration* of His Spirit;"[1] "Come, Holy Ghost, our souls *inspire;*"[2] "Grant . . . that by Thy holy *in-*

[1] Art. XIII.   [2] Veni Creator.

spiration we may think those things that are good;"[1] "Cleanse the thoughts of our hearts by the *inspiration* of Thy Holy Spirit;"[2] "Beseeching Thee to *inspire* continually the universal church."[3]

"I was in no wise called upon to attempt any definition of Inspiration," says Archbishop Tait, in his pastoral letter, "seeing that the church has not thought fit to prescribe one."

"The church has laid down," says the Archbishop of York, in his pastoral letter, "no theory of Inspiration; she has always had in her bosom teachers of at least two different theories."

"We heartily concur with the majority of our opponents," says the Bishop of Gloucester and Bristol, "in rejecting all theories of Inspiration."[4]

"Let us beware," says Dean Burgon, "how we commit ourselves to any theories of Inspiration whatever."[5]

"Our church," says Bishop Thirlwall, "has never attempted to determine the nature of the Inspiration of Holy Scripture."[6]

"If you ask me," says Dr. Cotton, Bishop of Calcutta, "for a precise theory of Inspiration, I confess that I can only urge you to repudiate all theories, to apply to theology the maxim which guided Newton in philosophy, *hypotheses non fingo*, and to rest your teaching upon the facts which God has made known to us."[7]

"It must be borne in mind," says the *Quarterly Review*, "that the Church Universal has never given any definition of Inspiration."[8]

"It seems pretty generally agreed," says the Bishop of Winchester, "that definite theories of Inspiration are doubtful and dangerous."[9]

---

[1] Col. 5th Sunday after Easter.
[2] Col. Communion Service.
[3] Prayer for the Church Militant.
[4] Aids to Faith, p. 404.
[5] Pastoral Office, p. 58.
[6] Charge, 1863, p. 107.
[7] Charge, 1863, p. 69.
[8] April, 1864, p. 560.
[9] Aids to Faith, p. 303.

VIII.

HIS DIVINITY.

" My crown is in my heart, not on my head."

AND so, it may be repeated, we stand upon the threshold of evidence just as we have reached its conclusion—as the mocking-bird stands upon the threshold of melody when it has sung its first song in the night, and the song is done; as the lover is only beginning a life of devoted proof when he has burst into the rapturous declaration, "Behold, thou art fair, my love; there is no spot in thee." It is in its supernatural, superhuman, divine ideas that the Scripture shows itself to be from God. It is as a piece of literature so far surpassing all other fruits of letters that everything else is driven out of comparison. It dwarfs all other books. It makes them dwindle into insignificance. It contains the most enduring laws, the most dramatic and vivid pictures of human character, the most graphic narrative, the sublimest poetry, the most powerful oratory. We call some men immortal because they live in the honor of posterity. But where are Justinian and Solon in comparison with Moses? Where are Homer and Virgil in comparison with Isaiah? And how shall Tennyson venture into the presence of David? The mighty Shakespeare, we are poetically told, "kissed all the shores of thought." But how shall all his sayings stand the flashing genius and profound wisdom of Solomon and all the prophets? Was ever human nature so pictured and portrayed in every motive of the heart and every movement of the life as in the Book of Psalms? The secrets of the soul are there laid bare. The springs of human thought and feeling are there uncovered. Let any man of any condition at any time pick up at random that marvellous collection of songs, and there he will find the echo of his transitory thought and there the image of his deepest feeling. Was drama ever so loftily conceived and so masterly sketched, and written, as it were, "with an iron pen in the rock forever," as the drama of the Book of Job? Of all the books that have ever been written, says Carlyle the seer, the Book of Job shall become, as time goes on, and history is unfolded, and men grow into more vivid intellectual life and spiritual apprehension, "all men's book." Its stage is the universe; its setting is the spheres; its passion is of the heart of all humanity; its philosophy is from eternity; its spirit is from the four great winds; its inspiration is of God. And as for pictures, neither Raphael nor Correggio nor Vandyke nor Titian ever painted with so swift or sure a hand as did those artists of the olden time, those masters of their craft, who drew the pictures of prophets and of kings to hang in the world's gallery forever. The delineators of human character, whose names have been enrolled in the great academy of the hearts of millions, are happy in their fame and love. So we honor for their genius, and we love for the stories they have told, the great dramatist of Stratford, the new creator of "Vanity Fair," the father of Copperfield and Pickwick, the "Wizard" of Rebecca and Meg Merrilies, the men across the stormy Channel who have given us "Les Miserables," the "Comédie Humaine," and "The Downfall." But the men who have given us Abraham and Joseph and Moses and David; the men who have drawn Elijah and Isaiah; who have delineated Peter and John and Paul; who have sketched with exquisite touch the gentle figures of Ruth and Mary; who have told us the pitiful yet precious story of the Magdalen—these are the Immortals of immortals. With few and telling strokes the living figures have risen under the divinely guided pen. Saul is there—in their peopled pages—in his majesty and madness; and Esther in her beauty and her passion. Judas is there in his treachery and despair. Jonathan is there in his gentle love and unfailing loyalty; and Cornelius the centurion, whose prayers and alms had made an incense before the Jehovah of all nations. And "time would fail me to tell of Gideon, and of Barak, and of Samson, and of Jephthah; of David also, and Samuel, and of the prophets." Above them all, and overshadowing all, rises the gentle, lustrous, towering, kingly figure of the "Messiah the Prince," "cut off" "in the midst of His days." In His eyes is the love-light for the penitent sinner—"Go, and sin no more." In His flashing gaze is the burning of judgment—"Woe unto you, scribes and Pharisees, hypocrites!" And yet "His visage is marred more than any man," as He is "wounded for our transgressions" and "bruised for our iniquities"; and yet He is "fairer than the children of men"—the "King in His beauty."

Did ever one look into such a land of giants and of heroes! The knights of Arthur are but a pale reflection of attenuated myth to these men of flesh and blood. The gods of the "Iliad" and "Odyssey" are but ghostly phantoms. Go anywhere, in any civilized clime, and ask any man, prince or pauper, priest or publican, author, statesman, soldier, scientist, What is the greatest book that was ever written? There is but one answer, echoing through the visionless boundaries of time: the Bible, the Book of God.

"What a Book!" says Heine the poet. "Vast and wide as the world, rooted in the abysses of creation, and towering up beyond the blue secrets of heaven. Sunrise and sunset, promise and fulfilment, life and death, the whole drama of humanity, are all in this book! Its light is like the body of the heavens in its clearness; its vastness like the bosom of the sea; its variety like scenes of nature."

Says Professor Conant: "The gnomic poetry of the most enlightened of other nations will not bear comparison with it in the depth and certainty of its foundation principles, or in the comprehensiveness and moral grandeur of its conceptions of human duty and responsibility."

Ewald: "In this Book, in this Book is contained all the wisdom of the world."

Andrew Jackson: "That Book is the rock on which our Republic rests."

"I fear you are ill," said Dr. Latham to Faraday, whom he found in tears, with his hand resting on an open book. "It is not that," said Faraday, with a sob, "but why will people go astray when they have this blessed Book to guide them?"

Theodore Parker: "This collection of books has taken such a hold on the world as no other. The literature of Greece, which goes up like incense from that land of temples and heroic deeds, has not half the influence of this book. It goes equally to the cottage of the plain man and the palace of the king. It is woven into the literature of the scholar and colors the talk of the streets."

Professor Huxley: "How is the religious feeling, which is the essential basis of conduct, to be kept up in the present utterly chaotic state of opinion . . . without the use of the Bible? The pagan moralists lack life and color, and even the noble Stoic, Marcus Antoninus, is too high and refined for an ordinary child. By the study of what other book could children be so much humanized and made to feel that each figure in the vast historical procession fills, like themselves, but a momentary space in the interval between two eternities, and earns the blessings or the curses of all time according to its efforts to do good and hate evil?"

Hooker: "There is scarcely any noble part of knowledge worthy the mind of man but from Scripture it may have some direction and light."

Translators of 1611: "If we be ignorant, the Scriptures will instruct us; if out of the way, they will bring us home; if out of order, they will reform us; if in heaviness, comfort us; if dull, quicken us; if cold, inflame us. *Tolle, lege. Tolle, lege.*"

Why is it so? Why this unapproachable superiority? Why has this book become, as it has, the one great book of humanity for all the ages of human life—for the millions dead and the countless millions yet to come? This genius of these writers—is it hereditary? God pity us, then, that we have not its pedigree! Is it the evolution of literary power, bursting forth at the consummation of the ages as the crown of intellect, the perfect flower of the blossoming vine that hath its roots in the primal fountain of life? God pity, then, the degeneracy of these days! Then is "The Rape of the Lock" but the lisp of numbers. The story of "Childe Harold" is only the prattling of an infant. "Lear" and "Hamlet" are but the ravings of one "who hath no speculation in his eye," or the drivellings of "a mind diseased." "The Idyls of the King" are only idle vaporings of a pitiful dreamer who hath not sense to see in his thin verse the slow decay of poesy. Galileo and Newton are wrecks of Joshua and Moses, for neither could Galileo conceive that the sun should stand still on Gibeon, nor Newton originate the idea of the awful Power that would throw back the gravity of worlds, and brush aside the waters of the deep Red Sea. Oxford and Heidelberg are but the grammar-schools of Jericho and Jerusalem, and the belles-lettres of Elizabeth and Victoria are primer compositions to those of Ezra, Herod, and the early Cæsars. But the ages are not consummated. Learning is increased. Literature is developing to its triumphs while the world is multiplying its authors and constantly raising the magnitude of its stars of genius. Egypt and Babylonia were more cultivated than Judah; yet nowhere outside of Israel in the ages that brought to light the sacred books was there a parallel authorship. The Bible is unique in human composition. It strikes the law of mental evolution to the heart. It stands forever as a divine anachronism in literature. Did it come from man? Then the men were not men, but demigods—and more. For they wrought chaos in the laws of human thought. They pulled down every principle of human composition, overthrew the edifice of natural learning, blotted out the constellations in the literary skies, crushed the world of learning into fragments, and launched into the dim abysses of space "new heavens and a new earth." They "spake, and it was done"; they "commanded, and it stood fast." Or else the Bible is a miracle of sacred thought and passion. For its thought is above all human thought, "higher than the heaven is above the earth;" and its passion of love "passeth knowledge."

It hath in it elements that pierce the soul. It is full of God and righteousness. To the soul of man in his ignorance, his speculation and doubt and infidelity; to the soul in its sorrow, its wretchedness and sin; to the soul in its longings and thirstings and tremulous aspirations; to the intellect and genius of mankind; to the mind in its wealth or its poverty; to every man—there is none left out—to his deepest, strongest, highest nature, in his weakest, hopeless, and expiring moments, it speaks of God. Before his frail and failing body, his loss of power as years and ailment lay their awful weight upon him; before the endless progression of change which he witnesses in himself and in the world, as youth and manhood deaden into decay, as friends are shifting and passing away, and dropping out of life and into silence; before the wrecks of fortunes and the overthrow of governments; before the sweep of fashions and the sway of new-born theories, amid the passing panorama of the whole world's restless and ever-changing history; before the fall of hopes into the abyss of night, and the fall of the heart's beloved into the fathomless grave; before the blotting out of worlds which thus become the awful prophecies of the final "crash of matter and the wreck of worlds," it tells of God.

> "Thou, Lord, in the beginning hath laid the foundation of the earth,
> And the heavens are the works of thy hands:
> They shall perish; but thou continuest:
> And they all shall wax old as doth a garment;
> And as a mantle shalt thou roll them up,
> As a garment, and they shall be changed:
> But thou art the same,
> And thy years shall not fail."

HIS DIVINITY. 83

Among all the theologies of man, with their definitions and formulas, with men plunged in mysterious longing to know God, was there ever sublimer and more comforting idea of Him than this:

> "Jehovah, Jehovah, a God full of compassion and gracious, slow to anger, and plenteous in mercy and truth; keeping mercy for thousands, forgiving iniquity and transgression and sin; and that will by no means clear the guilty."
>
> "Thus saith the high and lofty One that inhabiteth eternity, whose name is Holy: I dwell in the high and lofty place, with him also that is of a contrite and humble spirit, to revive the spirit of the humble, and to revive the heart of the contrite one."
>
> "For thou art our Father, though Abraham knoweth us not, and Israel doth not acknowledge us: thou, O Jehovah, art our Father; our Redeemer from everlasting is thy name."
>
> "Surely he hath borne our griefs, and carried our sorrows: yet we did esteem him stricken, smitten of God, and afflicted. But he was wounded for our transgressions, he was bruised for our iniquities: the chastisement of our peace was upon him; and with his stripes we are healed."

Was there ever any gentler, juster, more divine law than this, in the Book of the Covenant: "Ye shall not afflict any widow, or fatherless child. If thou afflict them in any wise, and they cry at all unto me, I will surely hear their cry." If a neighbor's garment is taken in pledge it must be returned before sundown, "for it is his only covering: . . . wherein shall he sleep? and it shall come to pass, when he crieth unto me, that I will hear; for I am gracious." Thus it is, to the weak and helpless, the stranger, the widow, the orphan, the poor, the slave, God's law is ever strong and tender. So says Professor Huxley: "The Bible has been the *Magna Charta* of the poor and of the oppressed; down to modern times no state has ever had a constitution in which the interests of the people are so largely taken into account, in which the duties so much more than the privileges of rulers are insisted on, as in Deuteronomy and Leviticus; nowhere is the fundamental truth that the welfare of the state depends on the uprightness of the citizen so strongly laid down."[1]

God's warnings are clear and true and strong, and His anger is terrible, but His judgments are tempered with mercy. "His wrath endureth but the twinkling of an eye; but in His pleasure is life." "Mercy and truth are met together; righteousness and peace have kissed each other."

> "Ye that put far away the evil day, and cause the seat of violence to come near; that lie upon beds of ivory, and stretch themselves upon their couches, and eat the lambs out of the flock, and the calves out of the midst of the stall; that sing idle songs to the sound of the viol; that devise for themselves instruments of music, like David; that drink wine in bowls, and anoint themselves with the chief ointments: but they are not grieved for the affliction of Joseph."
>
> "Forasmuch therefore as ye trample upon the poor, and take exactions from him of wheat: ye have built houses of hewn stone, but ye shall not dwell in them; ye have planted pleasant vineyards, but ye shall not drink the wine thereof. For I know how manifold are your transgressions and how mighty are your sins; ye that afflict the just, that take a bribe, and that turn aside the needy in the gate from their right."
>
> "O thou seer, go, flee thee away into the land of Judah, and there eat bread, and prophesy there; but prophesy not again any more in Bethel."
>
> "Hear the word of the Lord, ye children of Israel: for the Lord hath a controversy with the inhabitants of the land, because there is no truth, nor mercy, nor knowledge of God in the land. There is naught but swearing and breaking faith, and killing, and stealing, and committing adultery; they break out, and blood toucheth blood."
>
> "They feed on the sin of my people, and set their heart on their iniquity. And it shall be, like people, like priest: and I will punish them for their ways, and will reward them their doings."
>
> "I will heal their backsliding, I will love them freely: for mine anger is turned away from him. I will be as the dew unto Israel: he shall blossom as the lily, and cast forth his roots as Lebanon."

[1] Essays on Cont. Ques., p. 52.

"Let the wicked forsake his way, and the unrighteous man his thoughts: and let him return to the Lord, and he will have mercy upon him; and to our God, for he will abundantly pardon. For my thoughts are not your thoughts, neither are your ways my ways, saith the Lord."

The ceremonial law was of infinite detail. Times came when it overshadowed the homage and devoutness of the soul, times when it was formal and empty. But never was there truer and loftier spirit of worship than that which was fostered by this very code of the priests. Listen while the harp is struck and the strains come to us from the sweet singers of Israel:

"How amiable are thy tabernacles, O Lord of hosts! My soul longeth, yea, even fainteth for the courts of the Lord: my heart and my flesh crieth out for the living God."

"Like as the hart desireth the water-brooks, so longeth my soul after thee, O God. My soul is athirst for God, yea, even for the living God: when shall I come to appear before the presence of God? . . . I pour out my heart by myself; for I went with the multitude, and brought them forth into the house of God; in the voice of praise and thanksgiving, among such as keep holy-day. . . . O send out thy light and thy truth, that they may lead me, and bring me unto thy holy hill, and to thy dwelling. And that I may go unto the altar of God, even unto the God of my joy and gladness; and upon the harp will I give thanks unto thee, O God my God."

"What is there," says one [1] whose name is a watchword among Christian thinkers, ". . . which the Psalms are not able to teach? Heroical magnanimity, exquisite justice, grave moderation, exact wisdom, repentance unfeigned, unwearied patience, the mysteries of God, the sufferings of Christ, the terrors of wrath, the comforts of grace, . . . Providence over this world, and the promised joys of that world which is to come; all good . . . to be either known, or done, or had, this one celestial fountain yieldeth." Another,[2] one of the greatest geniuses in English history, says of David's

---

[1] Hooker, E. P., vol. ii., p. 159.
[2] Hero-Worship, Carlyle, p. 75.

history in the Psalms: "The truest emblem eve given of a man's moral progress and warfare here below . . . the faithful struggle of an earnest human soul toward that which is good and best. Struggle often baffled, sore baffled, down as into wreck; yet a struggle never ended; ever with tears, repentance, true unconquerable purpose, begun anew. . . . Is not man's walking in truth always that: a 'succession of falls'? In this wild element of life he has to struggle onward; now fallen, deep abased; and ever with tears, repentance, with bleeding heart, he has to rise again, struggle again still onward."

While the nations round about Israel were steeped in idolatry and superstition; while they were engraving perishable thoughts on imperishable stone and clay; while culture was lavish among them, and Israel was a new kingdom, with a shepherd lad upon the throne, such as these were the immortal songs of her people:

> "Have mercy on me, O God, after thy great goodness; according to the multitude of thy mercies do away mine offences. Wash me throughly from my wickedness, and cleanse me from my sin. For I acknowledge my faults, and my sin is ever before me. Against thee only have I sinned, and done this evil in thy sight; that thou mightest be justified in thy saying, and clear when thou art judged. . . . Turn thy face from my sins. and put out all my misdeeds. Make me a clean heart, O God, and renew a right spirit within me. Cast me not away from thy presence, and take not thy Holy Spirit from me. . . . The sacrifice of God is a troubled spirit: a broken and contrite heart, O God, shalt thou not despise."

> "Praise the Lord, O my soul: and all that is within me praise his holy name. Praise the Lord, O my soul; and forget not all his benefits. Who forgiveth all thy sin, and healeth all thine infirmities: who saveth thy life from destruction, and crowneth thee with mercy and loving-kindness. . . . The Lord is full of compassion and mercy, long-suffering, and of great goodness. He will not always be chiding; neither keepeth he his anger forever. He hath not dealt with us after our sins: nor rewarded us according to our wickedness. For look how high the heaven is in comparison to the earth: so great is his mercy also toward

them that fear him. Look how wide the east is from the west: so far hath he set our sins from us. Yea, like as a father pitieth his own children, even so is the Lord merciful unto them that fear him. For he knoweth whereof we are made: he remembereth that we are but dust."

"The Lord is my Shepherd; therefore can I lack nothing. He shall feed me in a green pasture, and lead me forth beside the waters of comfort. He shall convert my soul, and bring me forth in the paths of righteousness for his name's sake. Yea, though I walk through the valley of the shadow of death, I will fear no evil: for thou art with me; thy rod and thy staff comfort me. . . . Thy loving-kindness and mercy shall follow me all the days of my life: and I will dwell in the house of the Lord forever."

Rome became the empire of law and of statesmanship; Greece the land of art, of culture, of philosophy; but Israel was the nation of the highest letters, because it was the nation inspired with the genius of righteousness. Even her worldly wisdom, her sages and wise men, were clothed with God: "Behold, the fear of the Lord, that is wisdom; and to depart from evil is understanding."

"The Lord possessed me in the beginning of his way,
Before his works of old.
I was set up from everlasting, from the beginning,
Or ever the earth was.
When there were no depths, I was brought forth,
When there were no fountains abounding with water.
 .   .   .   .   .
There was I by him, as a master workman:
And I was daily his delight,
Rejoicing always before him;
Rejoicing in his habitable earth;
And my delight was with the sons of men."

And from this sublime idea there grew the still sublimer words: "In the beginning was the Word, and the Word was with God, and the Word was God. . . . All things were made by Him; and without Him was not anything made that hath been made. In Him was life; and the life was the light of men."

IX.

HIS EXALTATION.

"The purest treasure mortal times afford."

THE Bible tells us of God as the Living God. He is a Father, a Providence, a Deliverer; He is the Prince of Peace, the King of kings and Lord of lords, the Saviour and Redeemer. It gives us laws that are as enduring as time. It furnishes the eternal principles of righteousness, showing that right is right and wrong is wrong, and that these principles are older than any systems or any laws "written and engraven in stones." It shows that back of priests and ceremonials, back of Moses and the Mosaic code, back of Sinai and the two tables, there is law stamped upon the constitution of the earth, written among the blazing constellations of the sky, investing the heaving waters of the sea and the trackless sands of the desert and the towering mountain-ranges; spreading through the fair blue canopy of space and embracing the worlds and ages; penetrating and filling all human life and all other life from the first monad in the dim beginnings of matter to the Crown and living Prince of creation; a law springing out of the fountain of the Godhead, written among the eternities—a law of life and death, of hope and despair, of sin and of righteousness: "The wages of sin is death;" "The just shall live by faith." This law is not a Hebrew enactment. It is not a conceit of man. It is not a miraculous creation. All that the Bible tells us of it is merely the expression, the announcement to bewildered men, of the verities of the living universe. While men groped and stumbled and fell the light shined, and then men saw and stood erect and "walked and leaped, praising God."

2. There is evil in the world. Yes, the Bible sees it, and puts it down upon its pages; and it doth "naught extenuate." There is good in the world, yes, infinite good, measureless, unfathomable good in earth and sky, and the Bible crystallizes it, stereotypes it, builds it into its eternal pages, that it may stand a towering edifice forever. It is "longer than the earth, and broader than the sea." Its domes and pinnacles stretch above the sky and are hidden to man's failing vision beyond the clouds. The good and evil are forever contending, wrestling, struggling. Now virtue is triumphant, and now vice. In the whole universe of souls there is "a law" of the "members," "warring against" and sometimes "leading into captivity" the "better" and "higher" law of the "mind." There is moral disappointment and bitterness, and failure and disaster and catastrophe, from without and from within. What does it mean? How shall it all end? It is the great problem of problems. It faces men from the cradle to the grave. The master minds of all centuries have wrestled with it, and failed, and stood dumb and blind before it. It has defied analysis; it has wrecked reason. There is but one possible solution; one only that does not annihilate the principles of life and crush to atoms the foundations of the worlds: Good shall triumph finally. Death and hell shall be cast into the lake of fire. The dead shall burst above and trample underfoot the grave. God "shall wipe away all tears from out all eyes." "The living, the living"—they shall stand before God. And "the Lord God omnipotent reigneth."

Thus the Bible answers the "riddle of the ages," while Job bows himself over the ash-heap and curses the day that he was born; and finally surrenders speculation, and launches out once more into the boundless ocean of thought and life, secure in the ark of safety, ribbed about with the divine words, "I know that my Redeemer liveth, and that He will rise over the dust at the last. And after they have thus destroyed my skin, yet out of my flesh shall I see God: whom I shall see for myself, and mine eyes shall behold, and not another."

3. There may be blemishes in the Bible. But they are history, not revelation. They do not besmear the volume from leaf to cover. There are blemishes in men, but we do not cast them all into the pit. They are still the crown of terrestrial life, the princes of the earth. They have by divine right "dominion over the beasts of the field, and over the fowls of the air, and over the fishes of the sea." The Canaanites are slaughtered; but "the soul that sinneth, it shall die." David stole away his neighbor's wife and slew her husband in the "forefront of the battle"; but high above the iniquities of the sinning poet sound the rolling voices of Sinai: "Thou shalt not kill, Thou shalt not commit adultery."

Ecclesiastes may be cynical at times, but out of his cynicism grows the deep conviction of another life where right is triumphant. Out of it comes the tender warning, full of beauty and of power: "Remember now thy Creator in the days of thy youth." Out of it comes the sublime and simple rule of life for skeptics and believers together: "Fear God, and keep His commandments: for this is the whole duty of man."

The Psalms may now and then defile, as it were, their lips by muttering imprecations; but, as another has so beautifully said, they have become "the classic to all time of prayer and praise."

To reckless and evil-minded critics the Song of Songs may seem a voluptuous composition of a human hand, without a trace of God; but to the reverent scholar it is "the exquisite celebration of a pure love in humble life; of a love which no splendor can dazzle and no flattery seduce."

The Book of Jonah may or may not be history; it may be a divine fiction, like the parables of Christ; it is none the less a poem of divine beauty, teaching of the sin and repentance of men and prophet, and the tender mercy of the Father.

The Book of Daniel may or may not have been written by Daniel or in Daniel's time; but it shows us the figure of a godly hero, who, when he knew "that the writing was signed" decreeing death to any but idolaters, "kneeled upon his knees three times a day, and prayed, and gave thanks to God, as he did aforetime." It shows yet a brighter and diviner figure of "one like unto the Son of man," "like unto the Son of God;" of a kingdom "not of this world," a kingdom that is "for ever and ever," "wherein dwelleth righteousness."

The Apocalypse of John may be full of mystical and strange figures, lurid, ominous, blazing with a sulphurous light; but the Christian scholar may see in it "an inspired outline of contemporary history; . . . the tremendous manifesto of a Christian seer against the blood-stained triumph of imperial heathenism; a pæan and a prophecy over the ashes of the martyrs; the thundering reverberations of a mighty spirit struck by the fierce plectrum of the Neronian persecution, and answering in impassioned music which, like many of David's psalms, dies away into the language of rapturous hope." The soul of man, in any spot and in any time, may see therein the figure of Him on the white horse, going forth "conquering and to conquer." The souls of men everywhere, panting "as the stag panteth after the water-brooks," may hear the music of the voices of the skies saying, "The Spirit and the bride say, Come. . . . And let him that is athirst come. And whosoever will, let him take the water of life freely."

4. Whence come these mighty thoughts, these lofty, moving sentiments, these trumpetings of irresistible and redeeming truth? In the sacred history and narrative, in laws and prophecies, in poems and parables, in the cold calculation of premeditated proverb and the bursting flame of impetuous and exultant song. They are only there—in The Book. They are not elsewhere. Take the choice sayings and productions of any other set of writers in any age, gather together the devoutest and most brilliant compositions of the choice preachers of the world to-day, and see if any of them would

dare to venture to take rank with, could ever hope to enter into, the leaves of The Book. Reason as one will, it seems a folly and a blasphemy to entertain the thought. Are they inspired? If not inspired whence are they? Are they inspired? Let the word perish. They are of God!

5. Mark how these writings have come down to us; and how they have been bound together, not by the flimsy and materialistic elements of paper and of paste, not by the strong artistic skill of binders, with their implements of skin and clasp; bound by a unity of thought and sentiment and brilliant purposes that defies all criticism, that answers every doubt. How got the Bible here? How came it here as *one?*—a thousand bits of writing, the first and last perhaps two thousand years apart; written by historian and poet, king and priest, narrator, scribe, governor, prophet, publican, Pharisee, physician, and fisherman; high and low, prince and peasant, skilled and unskilled, learned and unlettered. Hath it come through the "fortuitous concurrence" of circumstances? Is it the "natural selection" of literature, completing its work two thousand years ago, and then forever vanishing among the lost forces of forgotten time? Has this sublimest and most potent power in all the mental and spiritual forces of the literary universe been annihilated? How doth the tree still stand, "all clothed in living green," with its umbrageous branches stretching over the continents, and its leaves "for the healing of the nations," while its roots are withered into dust, and its soil struck out of space down into the dark abyss of nothingness? Surely if we are men and not idiots, if reason hath not "fled to brutish beasts," there is a meaning super-customary, extra-historical, more than any other human circumstance that we have ever known, in the marvellous gathering and preservation of these books throughout the ages. There is a divine philosophy in their affiliation; there is a chemistry of heaven in their cohesion. That a divine Intelligence and Will and Purpose hath brought them into one, and held them there, is a reasonable conclusion. Otherwise they

are a prodigy of the divinest fairy-land, defying fleshly handling, and legally consistent only with the nature of dreams. That God exalted men to make them; that God filled men with surpassing intellectual and spiritual power to write them; that God marshalled the nations and ordered their march in time, and moulded history and controlled events, and shaped the course of time, and so with His omnipotent hand hath pushed these books together down the centuries, and holds them firm within His grasp before the millions of living men to-day, is comprehensible. But otherwise they are as the phantom pranks of the phantom deities about Olympus, or the one monstrosity of intellectual nature.

6. And then their unity of thought and structure. There is no alien book within the binding. The same foundation underlies each superstructure. Genesis and Revelation are as the opposing fragments of a broken ring—a ring of pure, fine gold, describing the eternal circle of the love and power of God. Psalms and Leviticus are the poem and its theme. Everywhere throughout the Bible sin is painted black, insidious, and damning. And everywhere is righteousness "a shining light, that shineth more and more unto the perfect day." Everywhere there is hope for the despondent, comfort for the sorrowing, strength for the weak, courage for the fearful, light to them that sit in darkness, consolation for the suffering, rest for the weary, life for those that are in the shadow of death. There is no temporizing; there are no false lights; there is no veiling of the truth. The city of God is built foursquare, as the cherubim of God came from the four quarters of the heavens. Right is ever right, and wrong is ever wrong. Sin is ever pain, and righteousness is joy and peace. False learning, fanatical and theological prejudice, dull ignorance, technical interpretation and misinterpretation may pit text against text and passage against passage, and wrest and wrangle language out of place, but the unity of God's book is indestructible and beyond assail. Its main idea is ever the same. Its main thought is ever consistent. It speaks forever for God

and suffering and wandering humanity, of truth and immortality and honor.

And the "river of water of life" flows out of this Eden of divine ideas "to water the garden." The stream of the Messianic prophecy runs through it all. In the first hour of guilt and pain the promise is made: "The seed of the woman shall bruise the serpent's head." We care not how critics and interpreters may strip away the verbal significance of those words. The underlying sentiment is one with the cry of the Redeemer from the throne: "Surely I come quickly." In the light of the divine history of the Christ the words have become a prophecy of Him if they were never meant to be. And so through all the book the living waters run. He is a prophet like unto Moses; a child born, and a son given; "The mighty God, The everlasting Father, The Prince of Peace;" the righteous Servant, the Man of Sorrows, on whom should be laid the iniquities of us all; "Messiah the Prince," "cut off, but not for himself;" "one like unto the Son of man," to whom is given an "everlasting kingdom"; the "Glory" of the second temple; the "Sun of righteousness"; the Son of God, the great I AM; the living, resurrected Jesus, who is "alive forevermore"; who "came to seek and save the lost"; who gave us the matchless, loving story of the prodigal; who in His matchless personality hath made men know how "Blessed are the poor in spirit: for theirs is the kingdom of heaven. Blessed are they that mourn: for they shall be comforted. Blessed are the meek: for they shall inherit the earth. Blessed are they which do hunger and thirst after righteousness: for they shall be filled. Blessed are the merciful: for they shall obtain mercy. Blessed are the pure in heart: for they shall see God. Blessed are the peacemakers: for they shall be called the children of God. Blessed are they which are persecuted for righteousness' sake: for theirs is the kingdom of heaven."

X.

HIS POWER.

> "This is thy work, Almighty Providence!
> Whose Power, beyond the stretch of human thought."

THE moral power of the Bible in the world is another portentous fact. In this nineteenth century of light and learning and science and sneering skepticism, in this nineteenth century of pride and disbelief and criticism, two hundred million copies of the Bible have issued from the printing-press. Voltaire had said that in a century from his day it would cease to be printed at all. Why this unprecedented issue? By what "selection" has the Bible been chosen, out of the ages, out of the countless myriads of books that are crowding the millions of the world's printing-presses, thus to be multiplied beyond the outermost limits of competition? The Bible has been translated into almost every tongue over the earth's surface. Written originally in Hebrew and Greek, it has passed over into Egyptian, Coptic, Arabic, Persian, Indian, Chinese, Japanese, Latin, Italian, Swiss, Dutch, German, Russian, Norwegian, Eskimo, French, English, Spanish, Portuguese, and a multitude of dialects and separate languages among the North American Indians, the numerous tribes of Africa, and the Polynesian and other islanders. Men from "every nation under heaven" may say of these writers, as the strangers at Jerusalem exclaimed under the pentecostal shower: "We do hear them speak in our tongue the wonderful works of God." And wherever it has been, wherever it is—in distant or present time, in torrid or frozen zone, on the mountain-tops or in the plains, on land or sea, in the palace of Victoria or in the mud-hut of her meanest subjects in the boundless forests of the Dark Continent, with the intellectual and the feeble-minded, with the great and strong, and with the poor and weak—it is a new force, a superior power, a power embracing and limiting within itself its own genera and species, a power that stands alone in reach and majesty in all the literature of the earth. It is a power that not only speaks of, but "makes for righteousness." It is a power that stirs men out of the stagnant pool of slimy wickedness, and leads them to a sparkling fountain of a living virtue. If it were not inspired the veriest infidel could not deny that it hath ever been inspiring. Men have perverted it in this day and in past centuries, and made it the excuse of passion and of crime. They have persecuted and tortured and assassinated in its name. They have distorted its commands into instruments of heinous cruelty and hypocrisy. So men did make Jesus Christ, the innocent and lofty, the pretext for their bloody thirst. But the Bible has ever been the greatest of all instrumental powers for good. It has inspired men to nobler and grander lives. It has made the greatest heroes in history. It has blessed and purified the soil and atmosphere of human life in every civilized land. It has disbanded armies and prevented war. It has taken away the bloody, brutish appetites of men who fed on men. It has stopped the Roman patrician when he would have exposed his suffering infant to the eagle and the fox. It has stayed the hand of the Fiji savage when she would crush her children's heads against the jagged rock. It has made the world pitiful and tender to the maimed and halt and blind, to innocents and imbeciles, to the aged and infirm, to men so loathsomely diseased that they became a walking pestilence. It has lifted the drunkard out of the fiery lake in which would perish his imperishable soul. It has led the robber and the murderer out of the midnight of their crimes into the pure light of pardon and reform. It has made men chain the devils which infested them. It has washed away the foulness of the ancient and the modern Magdalen, and clothed her in the white robe of righteousness. It has built up character until it has become a towering monument of purity and shining strength. The greatest intellects have bowed before it in grateful homage; the humblest slave has looked up to it and found liberty and dignity of soul. It has blessed and elevated society, and wrought its power in civilization, governments, and thrones. It has given to men the courage and the grandeur of the gods; nay, it hath given them the courage and the grandeur of redeemed humanity; because it has given them the inspiration of an unearthly faith, through which they have "subdued kingdoms, wrought righteousness, obtained promises, stopped the mouths of lions, quenched the violence of fire, escaped the edge of the sword, out of weakness were made strong, waxed valiant in fight, turned to flight the armies of the aliens. Women received their dead raised to life again: and others were tortured, not accepting deliverance; that they might obtain a better resurrection: and others had trial of cruel mockings and scourgings, yea, moreover of bonds and imprisonment: they were stoned, they were sawn asunder, were tempted, were slain with the sword: they wandered about in sheepskins and goatskins; being destitute, afflicted, tormented; of whom the world was not worthy."

Are these the signs of Inspiration? Put the word aside, and ask another question: Are these the signs that these high thoughts of sacred penning, that this unearthly, spiritual force of sentiment came from God? Here is the summing up of evidence: men believed that they wrote by the special power of God; the Jewish nation and the Christian world believed it; the writing constitutes the most marvellous literature that the world has known; its gathering together and preservation seem a miracle of heavenly purpose; the noble thought, the lofty grandeur of the books are incomparable; the unity of the Bible is the wonder of all ages; its spiritual and moral power are unique, tremendous, boundless.

Is this the evidence of Inspiration? It is majestic and convincing evidence of something. We need not care for technicalities and definitions—the Bible is greater than them all. We need not care for biblical mistakes and inaccuracies —they are not so much as the wart on Cromwell's nose; the giant Protector was still there, and the wart was on his outermost projection. The Bible writers never claimed infallibility of ink and pen-point. They never claimed infallibility against infinitesimal kinks in the thread of Hebrew history, or dust-flecks on the Jewish statistics.

The Bible is, however, an infallible guide to life and righteousness, to immortality and eternal joy.

It is inspired—if theologians will insist upon the word— because it is made of God. The breath of God is in it— supernaturally, not contra-naturally. How men wrote, when they wrote, what they wrote with, what were their physical attitudes and their mental analyses at the time, are neither here nor there. These are but trifles—fringings on the outer skirts of investigation. The Bible finds men and controls them. It rescues them and glorifies them. It teaches truth, transcendent and eternal.

This is the Bible's own unique, exclusive power!

It makes no difference if it be natural or supernatural, if it be developed in history or flashed forth from the skies. It is an awful and sublime power, here in human life, come down to us, seen, felt, exalted, enthroned.

Now where do the great powers here present in the world come from? "God spake once; and twice I have also heard the same; that power belongeth unto God."

Pick up a stone, a "smooth" stone out of the "brook," if you will. It is hard. It is enduring. Hurl it against the Sèvres vase upon the antique stand, and nothing will be left but the broken fragments and the "scent of the roses." Sling it against the Philistine's forehead, and it sinks into the springs of life and chokes them. This is the stone's power. Or the great stone from the quarry has power to uphold a temple or a palace. Or it supports the "everlasting hills."

Go out amid the golden grain in harvest-time, and see it sported as the plaything of the winds, and watch the harvester as he builds it into pyramids of treasure, and see it threshed and fanned and gathered into barns. It is the "staff of life." It feeds the prince and the beggar; it strengthens man and beast. This is the power of wheat. It has its kindred grains. It is a petty king in the great vegetable kingdom. And the power of all the kingdom is the power of giving fleshly life.

Go into the sculptor's studio while he points the magic chisel against the solid stone, and the hammer falls, and the fragments fly as they will. Little by little, and inch by inch, through the sightless grain the iron is driven, while the statue grows. This is the power of human skill and genius.

In the springs and rivers, in the clouds and air, in the hills and valleys, in the land and sea, in the climate and soil, in the birds that fly and the fish that swim, in the insect that crawls and in the beasts that spring and leap, in different lands and different times, in all animate and inanimate nature, in the various endowments of mankind of skill and intellect, of reason, imagination, conscience, science, philosophy, oratory, art, and letters, there are different, varying, and specific powers. And surely they were all born of God. They did not originate of themselves; they were not the inventions or creations of man. They came from the eternal and all-reaching Power beyond the realm of vision and of intellectual chemistry, the Power that underlies and overshadows the spheres. So said the father of Greek philosophy: "God is in everything." It is not pantheism; it is the devout recognition of the divine omnipresence, and that "every good and every perfect gift cometh down from the Father of lights." It is the acknowledgment of the divine influence.

Now Inspiration, stripped of technicalities and definitions and theologisms, and of the prejudices and fanaticisms that have surrounded it, is nothing more nor less than *the divine influence*. In theology it has been crushed and bound into extremely narrow limits, and confined to very narrow functions. In very fact and truth it is expanded through the universe of God. It is the influence of God which has been many times expressed within the sacred books by words that signify to us a wind, or breath, or spirit. It is this that in the dim beginnings "moved upon the face of the waters." It is this that seized upon the wayward will of Saul. It is this that Job declared was in his "nostrils." It is the same word that describes a "perverse spirit," a "spirit of jealousy," an "evil spirit," a "spirit of all flesh," a "spirit of the beast that goeth downward to the earth," the "four spirits of the heavens." Even the lowest and malign spirits are proclaimed to have their original power from God. It is the word *ruach* in the Hebrew. It has a high sense. It means the Spirit of God. It means the power of God in the divine nature. But it also means the power of God in man and beast, and in the winds of heaven. The power varies, of course, in the various creatures. It hath endless and countless manifestations. It cannot be the same in the beasts and in the bushes, in the flower and in the family, in the rocky heights and in the soul of man. But the breath of God is in all nature as well as in the prophets and The Book: "By the word of the Lord were the heavens made; and all the host of them by the breath * of his mouth;" "There are diversities of gifts, but the same Spirit." All things are inspired because they have in them the breath, or power, of God. All men are inspired because the Spirit of God quickens and wooes the soul of every one: "There is a spirit in man: and the inspiration of the Almighty giveth them understanding." It is not enough to say that the word which describes the "Spirit" of God is not the same as that which describes the "breath" of life—that *ruach* means a living spirit, and *n'shamah* an animal breath; because the former is used in the same sense as the latter, and sometimes in a lower

* *Ruach.*

sense. It was *ruach* that Job had in his nostrils, and *n'shamah* that God breathed into Adam's nostrils; and *ruach*, again, that Job describes as "the breath of all mankind," and *ruach* that the Preacher calls "the spirit of the beast." It is not amiss, therefore, to use the gift to Adam of a living soul as a parallel to the inspiration of the prophets. It is not amiss, amid the "differences of administrations" and "diversities of operations," to say that "it is the same God that worketh all in all."

"Inspiration" is a metaphor. But metaphors stand for something. Inspiration stands for the eternal power and influence of God. It has a universal application. But in the distributions of the power it has its special applications. And so, in Christian thought, it stands especially for the righteous, spiritual influence of God upon the prophets and The Book. The man is nothing and the book is nothing apart from the power of God. But God touched them, He spoke to them, He blew upon them, He breathed into them—all metaphors become aflame at the radiance of the divine Presence—and they were invested with God's unique religious power over the souls of men. This is the meaning of Inspiration, in its divine simplicity, untrammeled and unclouded by systems and definitions. This is the meaning bursting through the metaphor and abounding. It is a meaning in which Judea and Christendom have been united while they knew it not. It is a meaning ever accepted by the conscience of God's people, though their consciousness may not have been awake to it. It is a meaning that no science nor criticism nor infidelity can ever challenge successfully, whatever they may add to it, because it is witnessed by all history and observation and experience. The dumb, dead, natural thing is swept by the breath of God, and it becomes instinct with a supernatural life and a divine potency.

In the stately Cathedral of St. Paul, in London, English gratitude placed a monument to the memory of the great Duke of Wellington. It has been called "the triumph of

English sculpture." The warrior was dead, and therefore his effigy, in bronze, reposes, on a massive sarcophagus. Above it is supported a marble canopy, with a bronze group at either end. In one Truth tears out the tongue of Falsehood. In the other Valor tramples Cowardice underfoot. The pure, exalted vigor with which these fair, draped women overcome these foul, nude men, the bitter anguish and the cringing meanness which the Vices suffer, are vivid and alive. Yet they are only bronze—a dumb and lifeless metal. The sculptor breathed his spirit into them, and they are clothed with life and power.

History tells us that another Sculptor worked, in some far-distant age, perhaps upon a plain of fragrant verdure in the land of Babylonia. There were no models there. There was no form in earth or sky to image forth the figure to be made. But the skilful hands dipped into the rich red clay and shaped its plastic substance in the twinkling of an eye. The limbs were straight and roundly molded; the trunk was raised upon them in graceful, massive strength; the head was set aloft, a paragon of manly beauty. Beneath the outer surface of the figure lay, in easy attitude, skein upon skein of sinewy muscles, and a fairy network of deep-blue veins showed through. No statue of Apollo Belvedere, or Moses after Michelangelo, could ever rank with this. It was at once the beginning and the mastery of the sculptor's art. It seemed as though it were the likeness of a god—so firm and strong and full of grace, the mouth; so shapely, delicately molded, fair, and ready for the awakening of a king, the eyes; so high, majestic, full of power, the brow, rising as a montain-peak of intellectual excellence. But it was only clay. It was not dead, for it had never lived. The masterpiece of ages, yet wasted in the wilderness. At once the glory and the pity of creation. But then a subtle influence spread over the clay. A thrill shot through the matchless form. It trembled. And the godlike eyes were opened. The lord of earth was living! "And the Lord God formed man of the dust of the ground, and breathed into his nostrils the breath of life; and man became a living soul."

So all the stars and skies and all the breathing multitudes are by the inspiration of the Spirit of the great Creator.

So, in those pages so divine and beautiful, so full of all the best and holiest power, there is, profoundly and preëminently, the Breath of God.

www.ingramcontent.com/pod-product-compliance
Lightning Source LLC
Chambersburg PA
CBHW030406170426
43202CB00010B/1516